Turquoise Mosaics

from Mexico

Turquoise Mosaics from Mexico

Colin McEwan, Andrew Middleton,
Caroline Cartwright & Rebecca Stacey

With contributions by
Adrián Velázquez, Maria Eugenia Marín,
Theya Molleson and Helen Liversidge

THE BRITISH MUSEUM PRESS

© 2006 The Trustees of the British Museum

First published in 2006 by The British Museum Press
A division of The British Museum Company Ltd
38 Russell Square, London WC1B 3QQ

Colin McEwan, Andrew Middleton, Caroline Cartwright
and Rebecca Stacey have asserted the right to be identified
as the authors of this work.

A catalogue record for this book is available
from the British Library

ISBN-13: 978-0-7141-2569-5
ISBN-10: 0-7141-2569-5

Designed and typeset in Minion and MetaPlus by Harry Green
Printed in China by C&C Offset Printing Co., Ltd

Contents

Director's Foreword

The turquoise mosaics from Mexico in the British Museum's collections are rare and unusual objects with a fascinating history. That they have survived at all is often due to fortuitous circumstance and the curiosity of nineteenth-century antiquarians and collectors. Most important of these was Henry Christy, a great benefactor of the Museum. Some mosaics are said to have been found in jewellers' workshops in Florence. There they were being systematically dismantled so that the tiny polished mosaic tesserae could be redeployed in other more fashionable ornaments. Although surely not fully understanding exactly what was before them, Christy and other collectors were nonetheless sufficiently impressed to acquire and eventually bequeath often unique artefacts to the Museum.

There are tantalizing hints of how these mosaics came to European shores. In 1519 the Aztec emperor Motecuhzoma is reported to have despatched an envoy bearing precious gifts for the bearded stranger Cortés and his entourage. It was in the course of the voyages of Cortés and others that many objects are likely to have found their way to the cities and royal courts of Europe. In the 1520s Albrecht Dürer is said to have seen and commented on exquisite pieces recently arrived from Mexico. Many turquoise mosaics were preserved in cabinets of curiosity and museum displays. Removed from their original contexts, however, the mosaics lost their cultural contexts and their ties with the people who originally made and used them. This book undertakes the challenging task of restoring meaning and understanding to an exceptional body of artefacts.

By bringing the combined skills and resources of the Museum's scientists to bear on the analysis of materials and construction, striking new insights have emerged. Historical research was begun by Elizabeth Carmichael and published in *Turquoise Mosaics from Mexico* (1970), which has long been out of print. New research has been combined with images gleaned from the codices and recently excavated finds of turquoise mosaic items from the Templo Mayor in Mexico City. Other finds from cave sites in the state of Puebla add valuable new data. Together these ensure that the results of the scientific study of the objects will be of keen interest to a wide audience. This research underscores the Museum's mission as a site of universal study where science, art and religion come together in a fruitful and fascinating dialogue.

I am most grateful to the Sosland Family, Kansas City, and to the Reed Foundation, New York, for their generosity in making this publication possible.

NEIL MACGREGOR

Acknowledgements

We are indebted to many colleagues who have given generously of their time and expertise in the preparation of this book. For the provision of information and illustrative materials, much of it not previously published, we thank Frances Berdan, Warwick Bray, John Pohl, Sue Scott, Richard Townsend and Phil Weigand. Frances Berdan, Sue Scott, Warwick Bray, Phil Weigand, Gordon Brotherstone and Elizabeth Carmichael all read drafts of the text and we are grateful for their insightful comments. In addition, Kathleen Berrin, Bob Cobean, Louise Durbin, Virginia Fields, Marie Gaida, Leonardo Lopez Lujan, Simon Martin, Saburo Sugiyama, Karl Taube and Marcus Winter helped to facilitate contacts and supplied valuable information and suggestions. We are especially indebted to Elizabeth Boone and Emily Umberger for their detailed and constructive comments on the text.

Our thanks go to Hilary Taylor, who facilitated our contact with couriers, curators and conservators at the close of the Royal Academy *Aztecs* exhibition. For wood samples Caroline Cartwright thanks the Jodrell Laboratory, Royal Botanic Gardens, Kew; for the provision of samples of resin Rebecca Stacey thanks Frances Berdan; and for resin and plant samples Caroline Cartwright and Rebecca Stacey thank the Economic Botany Centre and the Lower Nursery at Kew.

David Hoxley drafted the map, and the designs on several of the mosaics were clarified by Garth Denning's drawings: we thank them both. Thanks are due to the British Museum's Photographic Service, notably Anthony Milton, Saul Peckham, Mike Row and Trevor Springett. We acknowledge the help provided by colleagues in the Department of Africa, Oceania and the Americas, Stewart Watson and Stewart Marsden in particular, and also the assistance of scientists in the Department of Scientific Research at the British Museum. We thank Jonathan King and Sheridan Bowman for their support of this project. Special thanks go to Antony Simpson for his patient drafting and re-drafting of many illustrations. We are grateful to the team at British Museum Press: Isabel Andrews, Teresa Francis, Beatriz Waters and Charlie Mounter. Harry Green's design talent and skills are evident at every turn and we deeply regret his untimely passing.

The publication would not have been possible without the financial support of the Sosland Family, Kansas City, and, through the good offices of the American Friends of the British Museum, the Reed Foundation, New York, and we are most grateful for their generosity. Finally, we would like to acknowledge a debt to Elizabeth Carmichael, for without her prompting we would not have undertaken this new study.

1

Introduction

The nine turquoise mosaics in the collections of the British Museum have long attracted admiration for their masterful blend of technical skill and artistry. Combined with the fascination surrounding their association with ritual and ceremony, this makes them some of the most compelling objects in the Mesoamerican collections. The mosaics are a product of a long tradition in Mesoamerica of the use of stones and minerals including jade and turquoise, along with other precious materials such as gold, shells and brightly coloured feathers. Here we present a fresh description of them in the light of detailed scientific examination, together with insights into their construction and use.[1] By drawing on other earlier Mesoamerican mosaic traditions we also place them in their wider cultural and historical context.

Ancient Mexico

Although frequently described as 'Aztec', the style, materials and technology of the mosaics were influenced to some degree by those of earlier civilizations such as the Toltec, Zapotec and Maya (see figs 1 and 2). By the time of the Spanish arrival in 1519 much of non-Maya Mesoamerica had been incorporated into the powerful Aztec empire.[2] The Aztecs ruled from Tenochtitlán, an island metropolis, and maintained a dynasty based on military might coupled with long-distance trading and tribute networks stretching from the Caribbean to the Pacific. To the south of the Valley of Mexico the mountainous region of northern Oaxaca was occupied by the Mixtecs. From about AD 1200, through political alliances and military conquest, they had grown increasingly powerful and for a long time successfully resisted Aztec rule. Nevertheless, the Aztecs appear to have benefited from Mixtec skills in stonework and metalwork. Consequently the turquoise mosaics cannot easily be specified as 'Mixtec' or 'Aztec'; instead they are referred to as 'Mixtec/Aztec' or, simply, 'Mexican'.

Sources of information

The principal goal of this study is to show how the objects themselves constitute a rich repository of information. The materials employed, for example, reveal deep knowledge of the contemporary natural world and its resources as well as routes of trade, exchange and tribute. The effort involved in procuring the components testifies to their value and significance in a world imbued with myths and religious beliefs. Scientific examination and analyses have added to the histories of both the objects and the people who made

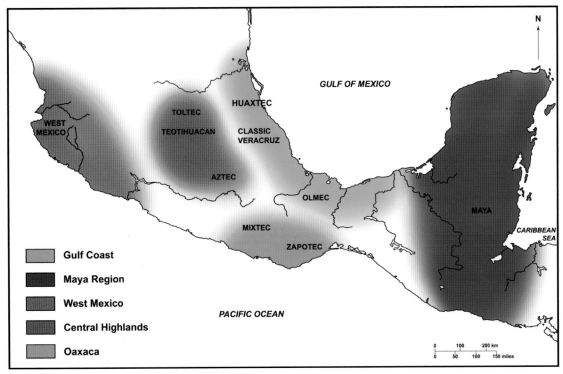

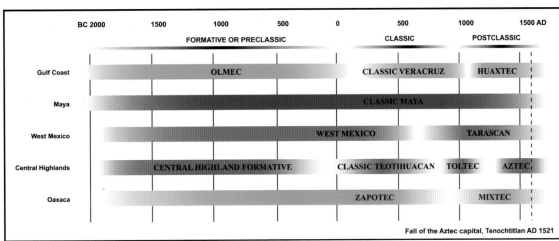

1 Map showing the regional distributions of the principal cultures of ancient Mesoamerica.

2 Timechart showing periods of maximum achievement and influence for ancient Mesoamerican cultures.

and used them. The mosaics provide evidence of the way that the materials were prepared, the methods of construction, the tools used and the choices that were made by artisans. The skill and technical knowledge invested in these remarkable objects shows how they were conceived and assembled. The deployment of unexpected materials sometimes reveals later modifications and repairs. Moreover, the spectacular mosaics that survive in museum collections today are victims of their later histories in that they have no direct archaeological provenance. Thus new mosaic finds from excavated contexts, despite their often fragmentary state, are vitally important for establishing and refining cultural associations.

A further source of information, not only on the mosaics and allied objects but on the materials and techniques of their construction, are the Codices – the Aztec and Mixtec histories recorded in painted images on paper, hide and cloth. There are around 160 Mexican codices, only a handful of which survive from pre-Columbian times, the others being the product of the tradition of painting histories that continued on into the colonial period.[3]

The early codices have been grouped according to their content and style. The principal groups are the Mixtec screenfold books, the Borgia codices and the Aztec cartographic histories. The screenfold books are Mixtec in origin and include the five undisputedly pre-Columbian codices: Bodley, Vienna Zouche-Nuttall, Becker I and Columbino.[4] These codices are genealogical histories that document the deeds of gods and ancestors, the founding of kingdoms, the dedication of religious festivals, and the diplomatic and military activities of key rulers (e.g. Lord 8 Deer) and subsequent dynastic genealogies. In contrast, the Borgia group, named after the famous Codex Borgia, deals with ritual beliefs and practices within calendrical cycles. Although Mixtec in style, the cosmology represented in these codices is pan-Mesoamerican, so their place of origin remains unknown.[5] The central Mexican cartographic histories are different; these map-based documents are primarily concerned with migration history and the founding of polities within the Aztec realm. Amid the complex iconography of all these documents, ritual accessories like the turquoise mosaic objects can be identified – masks, shields and knives. Moreover, they can be located in the customs and ceremonies in which they were employed and linked to the status of particular lineages, guilds or schools, such as eagle and jaguar warriors.

A wealth of information is also to be found in post-Conquest codices and accounts. The Codex Mendoza combines the pre-Columbian pictorial tradition with annotations (glosses) and commentary in Spanish.[6] Commissioned by royal officials and compiled by native scribes and informants in 1541–2, it documents the founding of Tenochtitlán, the subsequent imperial conquests by the Mexica (Aztec) rulers, and the tribute paid by the conquered communities. It includes a final section on 'daily life', recording the key events of birth and marriage, as well as details of the occupations of priests, warriors and other professions. Further important evidence comes to us from the writings of Friar Bernardino de Sahagún, whose sources were indigenous informants who had lived through the Spanish Conquest. In the twelve volumes of his *Historia de las cosas de Nueva España*,[7] also known as the Florentine Codex, he reports on all aspects of pre-Columbian Aztec life and culture, including crafts, skills, specializations and special offices, as well as plants, animals and the resources of the natural world. These accounts provide insights into the lives of people who created and used the mosaics, and help in understanding the choices they made in selecting their materials.

Other significant sources are Diego Durán's *Historia de Las Indias de Nueva España e Islas de la Tierra Firme* (*c*.1580),[8] and Peter Martyr's *De Orbe Novo* (1521).[9] Durán, a sixteenth-century Dominican friar, based his commentary on a now lost Náhuatl chronicle as well as interviews with informants. In contrast, Martyr records the region through personal interviews with Spanish explorers and inspection of the materials they brought back to Spain.

If these surviving documents and accounts set the scene for the world from which the turquoise mosaics emerged, the mosaics, in turn, showcase the skills and materials that the documents describe and are also a unique and spectacular material record of the ideology and ritual world they so lavishly depict.

Mosaics in the British Museum

Mosaics are well known as designs created from small pieces of different coloured materials such as marble, glass, shell or ceramics. The Mexican mosaics, although referred to as *turquoise* mosaics, actually comprise a wide array of other minerals including malachite, pyrite and lignite. Shells, such as conch and thorny oyster, were used in quantity, too; gold, resins and waxes also feature as design elements, while wood is the major structural material for most of the objects. The nine mosaics in the British Museum collections (fig. 4) include various masks, a knife, a ceremonial shield and a helmet. They all incorporate animal, human or deity elements in their design, and many of these features can be linked to the pantheon of Aztec gods. They are thought to have served principally ritual purposes and to have been worn or used ceremonially by priests or rulers.

The first printed report of Mexican mosaics appears in Peter Martyr's 1521 account of the early exploration of Mexico by Juan de Grijalva in 1518.[10] Some years later Oviedo refers to 'two masks of small stones like turquoise set over wood like mosaic'.[11] Grijalva is said to have obtained these masks by barter from the indigenous population of San Juan de Ulúa in Veracruz on the Gulf Coast of Mexico. An inventory of items similarly acquired by trade with other coastal settlements includes objects of gold, gilded and inlaid wooden artefacts and flint knives, as well as more examples of mosaics made from turquoise and other stones.[12] Soon after, the Cortés expedition (1519–26) culminated in the conquest of Mexico and resulted in considerable quantities of

3 Emissaries from Motecuhzoma meeting Cortés on his boat (Sahagún, Bk 12, pl. 3, ill. 12).

Mask of wood covered in turquoise mosaic with scattered cabochon turquoise producing the effect of 'warts'. Pierced mother-of-pearl eyes and shell teeth, h. 16.5 x w. 15.2 cm.

Double-headed serpent, possibly a pectoral. The mosaic is worked in turquoise and shell on carved wood, h. 20.5 x w. 43.3 cm.

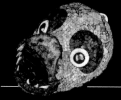

Animal head. Mosaic in turquoise and malachite. Mouth encrusted with gemstones and shark's teeth which, in addition to the pearls and glass used in the mosaic, are thought to be later modifications, h. 10 x w. 7.3 cm.

Skull, covered with turquoise and lignite mosaic, believed to represent the creator god Tezcatlipoca (Smoking Mirror), h. 19.5 x l. 12.5 x w. 12 cm.

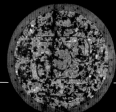

Shield with design in the form of the principal divisions of the Aztec universe, worked in turquoise and shell mosaic with gilded resin, diam. 31 cm.

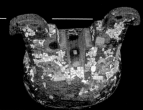

Helmet, with two 'horns', carved in wood with mosaic design depicting two entwined serpents, h. 22.3 x w. 20.5 cm.

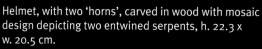

Jaguar bearing a shallow cup on its back. Carved in wood with turquoise and shell mosaic, h. 17 cm.

Knife with flint blade. The carved wood handle is in the form of a crouching eagle warrior. The mosaic is worked in turquoise, shell and malachite, h. 9.3 x l. 31.7 cm.

Mask depicting two entwined serpents, worked in different shades of turquoise. It is believed to represent the rain god Tlaloc, h. 17.3 x w. 16.7 cm.

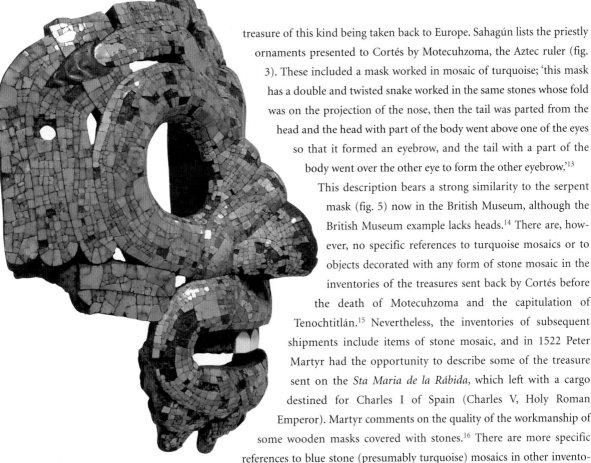

4 The nine turquoise mosaics in the British Museum collections.

5 Side view of turquoise mosaic mask with intertwined serpents.

treasure of this kind being taken back to Europe. Sahagún lists the priestly ornaments presented to Cortés by Motecuhzoma, the Aztec ruler (fig. 3). These included a mask worked in mosaic of turquoise; 'this mask has a double and twisted snake worked in the same stones whose fold was on the projection of the nose, then the tail was parted from the head and the head with part of the body went above one of the eyes so that it formed an eyebrow, and the tail with a part of the body went over the other eye to form the other eyebrow.'[13]

This description bears a strong similarity to the serpent mask (fig. 5) now in the British Museum, although the British Museum example lacks heads.[14] There are, however, no specific references to turquoise mosaics or to objects decorated with any form of stone mosaic in the inventories of the treasures sent back by Cortés before the death of Motecuhzoma and the capitulation of Tenochtitlán.[15] Nevertheless, the inventories of subsequent shipments include items of stone mosaic, and in 1522 Peter Martyr had the opportunity to describe some of the treasure sent on the *Sta Maria de la Rábida*, which left with a cargo destined for Charles I of Spain (Charles V, Holy Roman Emperor). Martyr comments on the quality of the workmanship of some wooden masks covered with stones.[16] There are more specific references to blue stone (presumably turquoise) mosaics in other inventories, for example 'a shield with blue stone mosaic-work' and 'a large head of a duck of blue stone mosaic-work',[17] so clearly a number of turquoise mosaics reached Europe in this period immediately after the Conquest.

The Mexican treasures were quickly dispersed around Europe. Certainly by 1521 some were in Brussels, where Albrecht Dürer recorded in a diary his impressions on seeing 'the things that were brought to the King from the land of new gold': 'All the days of my life I have seen nothing that has so rejoiced my heart as these things. For I saw among them strange and exquisitely worked objects and marvelled at the subtle genius of the men in distant lands.'[18] But Dürer's wonder on seeing these objects was not universal; indeed, it has been suggested that Dürer himself may have been more impressed by the monetary worth of so much gold and silver.[19] It seems clear that many items were broken up and reused in new settings or, worse still, melted down in order to realize their value as bullion. Many mosaics are thought to have been recycled in the *pietre dure* workshops of Florence in the early nineteenth century'[20] and this may account for certain modifications described in this book (see ch. 3). Against the odds some mosaics did survive in museums and in other collections and, in due course came to the notice of nineteenth-century collectors. Twenty-four mosaics were known in 1915: ten masks (with examples in Berlin, Copenhagen, Gotha, London, Rome, Vienna and Washington), five animals (Berlin, London and Vienna), one helmet (London), one double snake (London), one bone musical instrument (Rome) and one Xolotl figure (Vienna).[21] Most of these are thought to have been part of Spanish shipments soon after the Conquest,[22] and, apart from excavated examples, only one further mosaic has come to light in recent years – a mask of Tlaloc (fig. 6).[23] Newly excavated finds extend the list further. A recent collation of Mexican turquoise includes material such as beads and necklaces and a variety of inlaid items including pectorals, figures and ear ornaments from archaeological sites in Mexico.[24]

The British Museum's collection of mosaics began with the bequest by Henry Christy (1810–65) of three mosaics.[25] Later in the nineteenth century further mosaics were donated by Augustus Franks (animal head, helmet and jaguar) and three more were purchased (the shield, the serpent and the serpent mask).[26] In 1994 the nine mosaics were placed on permanent display in the newly designed Mexico gallery at the British Museum.

Antecedents in serpentine and jade

A range of raw materials was highly valued by all Mesoamerican cultures – in particular, stones exhibiting green and bluish-green hues which were sought as much for their symbolic importance as for their working properties. The procurement and trading of such materials played a vital role in evolving Mesoamerican civilizations. As early as the Formative period (2000–1200 BC) there is evidence for long-distance trading networks bringing in 'greenstone', jade and mica.[27] At this time serpentine and jade were dominant; turquoise is found only sporadically until about AD 700 and its use in mosaics is later still; some of the earliest evidence for turquoise mosaics is provided by the tesserae excavated from burials at the Late Classic, ceremonial site of Alta Vista (c. AD 400–850).[28]

The concept of using such materials to create a mosaic image emerges as early as the Middle Formative period (900–600 BC) at the Olmec site of La Venta on the Gulf Coast of Mexico.[29] Here three large mosaic pavements, each composed of several hundred blocks of dark green serpentine, were uncovered by excavation in the early 1950s. Located in the ceremonial precinct and intentionally buried after construction, the paved designs served as a kind of cosmogram marking the four world directions and

6 Turquoise mosaic mask of Tlaloc, AD 1200–1400, (h 18.5, w 16, d 9.2 cm).

underlining the role of the ceremonial centre as a pivotal, sacred space.[30] If this can be viewed as mosaic art on a grand scale, some of the defining features of the Meso-american mosaic tradition are already present, such as the use of composite designs to create symbolic images, the connection with sacred space and religious ceremonies, and the use of special and significant materials. Even earlier, small mosaics and bone fragments coated with red pigment have been recovered from a tomb at the Olmec site of Teopantecuanitlán (Early Formative 1400–500 BC) in Guererro.[31]

The Classic period (AD 250–600) saw the development of urban and ceremonial centres – among these, Teotihuacán, which by the early centuries AD was a city of perhaps 80,000 people.[32] It exerted economic influence over a wide area to the north-west, with trading links into what is now northern Mexico and south-west United States. There are indications that the trade in turquoise from south-west USA, for use in central Mexico, may have begun in the Early Classic.[33] There is some evidence for mosaic work at Teotihuacán in the form of a shell mosaic laid on a typical Teotihuacán black lime-stone mask,[34] and recent excavations at the Pyramid of the Moon have unearthed a

7 Façade of the Temple of Quetzalcoatl at Teotihuacán.

mosaic human figure among burial offerings.[35] The façade of the Temple of Quetzlcoatl at Teotihuacán features alternating sculptures of Quetzlcoatl and Tlaloc, the latter bearing mosaic-like headdresses (fig. 7).

In the southern highlands the rise of Teotihuacán was paralleled by the flourishing Zapotec civilization. Excavations at the Zapotec capital, Monte Albán, uncovered a jade mosaic mask, worn as a pectoral and dating to 150 BC–AD 100 (fig. 8). The piece is constructed from twenty-five dark green jade tesserae; highly polished, they fit neatly together to form a human face disguised as a bat, with eyes and teeth of shell.[36]

Examples of jade mosaics, in particular funerary masks, are also found throughout the Maya region of the Yucatán Peninsula during the Classic period.[37] Perhaps the most famous is the magnificent mask from the tomb of Lord K'inich Janaab' Pakal I at Palenque (fig. 9). This, together with a wealth of other jade accoutrements, preserves the image of the deceased ruler as an eternally youthful provider. Among

8 Zapotec pectoral in the form of a mask depicting the bat god. Classic, from Monte Albán (h 28, w 17.2 cm).

9 Jade mosaic mask from the tomb of Lord Pakal at Palenque (h 24 x w 19 cm).

the other naturalistic jade mosaics are the following: a mask believed to be from a Late Classic royal burial discovered in a tomb at Calakmul and another representing an unidentified Early Classic ruler from Tikal.[38] Also at Tikal a jade mosaic funerary vessel (fig. 10) with a portrait of Yik'in Chan K'awil or his son in the guise of the maize god was found in a Classic Maya temple burial.[39] A splendid example of the use of shell in mosaic work comes from a tomb at the Late Classic Maya site of Oxkintok. This is a pendant in the shape of a bird's head (fig. 11), an interesting precursor for the use of shell with turquoise on later mosaics.[40]

A Toltec mosaic-backed mirror, part of an offering uncovered in a columned building on the sacred precinct at Tula,[41] about 100km north of Tenochtitlán, is described as:

'34 centimetres in diameter and … formed by over 3000 small finely cut turquoise plaques along with scores of pyrite mosaic pieces.[42] Near the centre of the inferior section of the disc are two small holes with an indented area between them. These holes probably were used to attach the disc to the costume of some important personage.'[43]

The mosaics of turquoise and pyrite on the disc represent four Fire Serpents (Xiuhcoatl), and in the centre is a round pyrite mirror. The disc is probably

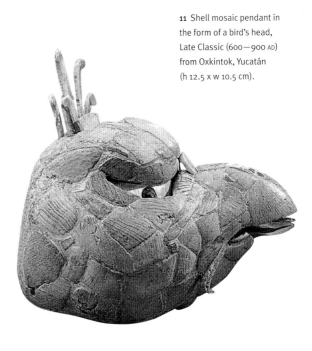

11 Shell mosaic pendant in the form of a bird's head, Late Classic (600–900 AD) from Oxkintok, Yucatán (h 12.5 x w 10.5 cm).

10 Jade mosaic funerary vessel with a portrait of Yik'in Chan K'awil of Tikal (h 25 x diam. 9 cm).

17

a ritual mirror, part of the costume of high-ranking warriors in various Mesoamerican cultures during the Classic and Post-Classic periods.[44] Similar turquoise mosaic discs have been recovered at the Post-Classic (AD 850–1150) Maya site of Chichén Itzá in the Yucatán peninsula, at the Templo Mayor (Great Temple) of Tenochtitlán (Mexico City), at Paquimé and in the Mixteca of Oaxaca.[45] At Chichén Itzá there are also relief sculptures depicting warriors wearing mosaic masks (fig. 12).[46] Similarly, a Late Post-Classic wall painting at Tulum depicts a figure with mosaic mask characteristic of the Aztec deity Tezcatlipoca (fig. 13; compare with the skull on p. 67). In both cases the mosaic material represented is unknown, but by the end of the Classic period (c. AD 900) the distribution of turquoise in Mesoamerica had broadened considerably and by the Post-Classic it had outstripped jade and was being traded into virtually every region.[47] Turquoise became the material of choice for the mosaics: several Zapotec examples have been excavated at the site of the Late Post-Classic (1100–1521 AD) city Zaachila.[48] and there are fine Post-Classic Maya examples of these, such as the mask in fig. 14 and the sceptre described on p. 19, which echo

12 Drawing of a relief sculpture at Chichén Itzá showing a warrior wearing a headdress and mosaic mask (after Maudslay, 1895–1902).

13 Drawn reconstruction of an interior wall painting from Tulum depicting a deity with mosaic mask, Late Post-Classic (after Miller 2001).

14 Turquoise mosaic mask on wood. Late Post-Classic Maya (h. 13.7 x w. 13.3 cm?).

the way the material is used in the Aztec-Mixtec objects that are discussed later in the following chapters.

The significance of materials

The combination of significant colours, materials and iconography in Mexican mosaics was intrinsic to their high status and the purposes for which they were made. A range of prestige materials was valued particularly for specific qualities such as their colour, translucence or reflective surfaces. Thus, the green colour of stones such as jade,

The sacred well, or *cenote*, at Chichén Itzá (fig. 15) is a natural feature, typical of the limestone landscape of the northern Yucatán. Formed by the collapse of a large underground cavern it opened up direct access to otherwise hidden subterranean streams and rivers. For many centuries it formed an important ritual focus and was the repository for a wealth of offerings, such as that shown in fig. 16, one of a number of sceptres or staffs that have been recovered during dredging of the well. The wooden staff is carved in the form of a 'diving' or descending figure. Traces of red pigment are visible around the eyes and more than a hundred jade and turquoise tesserae set in resin still adhere to the face. Diving or descent from the celestial sphere becomes an increasingly widespread theme in the Post-Classic period (see, for example, figs 20 and 96). This 'diving' figure descends holding balls in either fist that may represent copal (see fig. 46 and p. 36–7). It has been suggested that offerings of flaming, smoking copal hurled into the depths of the *cenote* might have represented celestial objects plunging earthwards to disappear into the underworld.[49] The vital characteristics of this artefact – the use of turquoise to create a mask-like face and emphasize its supernatural attributes – are extensively displayed in the Aztec/Mixtec mosaics described here.

15 The sacred *cenote* at Chichén Itzá.

16 Diving figure sceptre recovered from the sacred *cenote* at Chichén Itzá (l. 39, w. 8.1 cm).

amazonite[50] and serpentine carried connotations of moisture, vegetative growth and the perpetual cycle of renewal apparent in nature,[51] while metals like gold were revered for their reflective brilliance and warm colour.[52]

Gold was highly valued by the Aztecs: Sahagún describes it as 'perfection, the leader of all. It leads riches on earth. It is that which is sought, that which is desirable, that which is cherished, that which deserves being guarded, that which deserves being stored.'[53] Nevertheless, it was not as highly esteemed as the precious green and blue stones,[54] which would have been deliberately selected to signal the enduring other-worldly qualities of the subjects they portrayed, in mosaic or sculpture. This is exemplified in the Post-Classic Aztec sculpted bust of the Mexican creator deity

17 Stone bust of Quetzalcoatl, the Feathered Serpent, Post-Classic (h. 32.5 w. 23 cm).

18 Lord 8 Deer wearing the turquoise nose plug. Codex Zouche-Nuttall, p.77.

and culture hero, Quetzalcoatl – the Feathered Serpent (fig. 17).[55] The feathers are those of the quetzal bird, which boasts an extraordinary shimmering green-blue iridescent plumage.

With the import of larger quantities of turquoise to Mesoamerica the range of predominantly greenish colours of serpentine and jade was expanded to a rich new palette of aquamarine and blue-green colours. Across Mesoamerica turquoise soon became a hallmark of lordly divine status, and in central Mexico, as well as in the Yucatán, turquoise diadems were conferred on nobles of the highest rank. Words of wisdom were likened to turquoise, which came to embody fertility, rainfall, maize, the sky realm and themes of renewal of all kinds.[56] *Teoxiuitl*, the Náhuatl (Aztec/Toltec) word for fine turquoise, was formed of the suffix *teotl*, meaning 'god', and the root *xiuitl*, meaning 'turquoise' as a mineral, further emphasizing the esteem in which the stone was held. Sahagún tells of extravagant feasts held by the Aztec nobility to cement political allegiance and affirm strategic alliances, where turquoise figured conspicuously in the gifts that were exchanged and also formed part of the costumes of their 'bathed' slave servants: 'He [the nobleman host] put on heads of his bathed ones that were known as the *anecuyotl* … a turquoise device made with feathers' and 'he [the host] tied "shining hair strands" about their temples, which were decorated in this way: alternating [strips of] turquoise [and] gold, reddish coral shells [*Spondylus princeps*?], [and] black mirror stones.'[57] Turquoise is perhaps the most famous gift portrayed in the Mixtec codices; the turquoise jewel was awarded to

19 A conch shell trumpet-player leading a procession. Codex Magliabechiano, p.35.

20 Lady 3 Flint descends into water with a conch shell on her back. Codex Zouche-Nuttall, p.16.

Lord 8 Deer by the Tolteca-Chichimeca priest Lord 4 Jaguar.[58] This jewel (fig. 18) was inserted into the nasal septum of Toltec princes who had been elected to the position of a landholding prince who served as a lineage head. Turquoise also marked out the high status of artisans such as the *amanteca* (feather workers): 'Then he [a high-status feather worker] had placed on his radiating ornament of turquoise, his feathered staff, and his shield, his rattles, and his foam sandals.'[59]

Likewise marine shells had symbolic significance throughout Mesoamerican prehistory. Aside from their use as functional tools, some assumed the status of sacred objects such as conch trumpets (fig. 19). They were also worked into highly decorative beads, figurines and jewellery. They are routinely depicted in association with water. In the Mixtec codices, for example, conches feature frequently in events taking place in the watery locations illustrated in the Codex Zouche-Nuttall (fig. 20). Certain shells have immense symbolic significance – bivalve shells like the thorny oyster (*Spondylus*) and gastropods such as the conch (*Strombus*) are excellent examples. The red elements on *Spondylus* seem to have been particularly associated with blood and fertility. Both conch and thorny oyster shells appear together in the iconography of the sculpted façade of the Temple of Quetzalcoatl at Teotihuacán (fig. 21), reflecting their elevated status within Mesoamerican cosmology.

Although turquoise and shell are the principal prestige materials on the mosaics described here, many other materials were used with them to produce the finished objects. Some will have been invested with symbolic significance, while others such as wood and adhesives may have been selected for more practical properties such as workability or ease of procurement.

21 Shells depicted in the sculptures on the façade of the Temple of Quetzalcoatl at Teotihuacán.

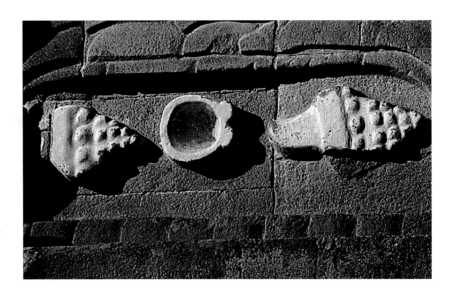

2

Mosaics under the Microscope

The new information at the heart of this book comes from the detailed scientific examination of the nine turquoise mosaics in the British Museum collections. This chapter introduces the materials procured and used in the construction of the mosaics, the scientific methods used to identify them, their qualities and how they were prepared and assembled by the Aztec/Mixtec artisans.

Microscopy and analysis: the science behind the art

Looking down a binocular microscope (fig. 22) at the turquoise mosaics brings the exquisite quality of the workmanship vividly to life. The magnified images (e.g. fig. 56) reveal the consummate skills of the Mixtec-Aztec craftsmen. This microscopic examination allowed identification of minerals and shells, but additional techniques were needed to identify other materials.

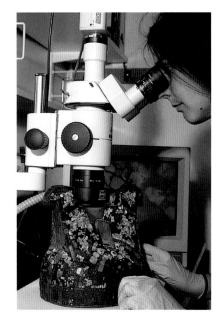

Non-destructive X-ray fluorescence (XRF; fig. 23) was used to confirm the presence of gold traces on the surfaces of some of the mosaics. Removal of minute samples of the gold foils in the decoration enabled examination and analysis with a scanning electron microscope (SEM) equipped with an energy-dispersive X-ray (EDX) analyser. In this way, the thickness of the foils could be measured and their composition determined (see ch. 3, p. 45). Mineral pigments used to colour some of the resins were identified using X-ray diffraction (XRD) or Raman microscopy. The Raman analysis was carried out directly on the object (fig. 24), while minute pigment samples were removed for the XRD analyses.

Sampling was also required for identification of the wood; again the samples were very small, less than one millimetre across, and were taken from already damaged areas. The samples were prepared by slicing them in the three planes necessary for accurate wood identification (fig. 25). Examination of the cut surfaces under a high-powered optical micro-

22 Examination of the turquoise mosaic helmet with a binocular microscope.

scope (fig. 26) reveals details of the cellular structure of the wood that is characteristic of the type of tree used. With this method the samples taken from the mosaics were then identified by comparison with known reference timbers (fig. 27).

Natural products, such as pine resin and beeswax, can only be identified from their chemical composition. Gas chromatography/mass spectrometry (GC/MS; fig. 28) was

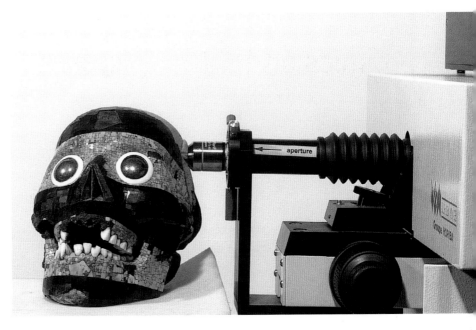

23 Analysis of tesserae on the helmet using X-ray fluorescence.

24 Using the Raman microscope to carry out direct analysis of the object.

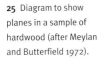

25 Diagram to show planes in a sample of hardwood (after Meylan and Butterfield 1972).

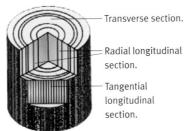

Transverse section.

Radial longitudinal section.

Tangential longitudinal section.

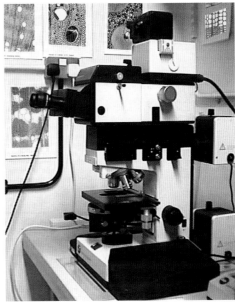

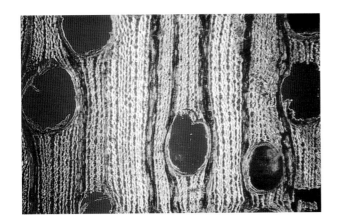

26 An optical biological microscope was used to reveal the cellular structure of the wood.

27 The characteristic transverse view of the cellular structure of the hardwood *Cedrela odorata*, as seen under the optical biological microscope in thin section.

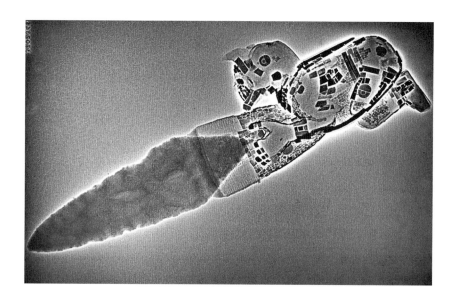

29 The knife with turquoise mosaic handle. The xeroradiograph reveals the blade inside the wooden handle.

28 Using gas chromatography/mass spectrometry (GC/MS) to identify resins and other amorphous organic materials.

used for this analysis[1], requiring minute sampling from already damaged areas. Crucial to understanding the techniques of construction was the employment of radiography, revealing features not visible on the surface. For example, the xeroradiograph of the mosaic knife (fig. 29) shows the position of the blade inside the knife handle.

Raw materials: selection and procurement

The Aztecs acquired a wide range of materials and luxury commodities via far-reaching trading links operated by *pochteca*, or long-distance merchants.[2] Some raw materials were supplied as tribute exacted by the Aztecs from subject territories, rather than coming directly by trade. While some materials may have reached the Valley of Mexico in an unworked state, it is likely that many came as finished or semi-finished components (e.g. cut and polished tesserae, fig. 30) or even as fully finished objects (e.g. masks, fig. 31). The focus here is on the range of materials examined on the mosaics in the British Museum collections.

TURQUOISE By far the most common mineral used is turquoise (fig. 32), a naturally occurring copper aluminium phosphate often containing some iron. The copper and iron are mainly responsible for the colour, which can be quite vivid or rather pale, and may vary from sky blue, through bluish green, to apple green (fig. 33). The full range of green-blue colours was exploited and different shades were often selected to accentuate particular design features.

The source of much of the turquoise used in ancient Mexico has long been thought to be the extensive high-quality deposits at Mount Chalchihuitl in the Los Cerrillos mining

30 A bowl of turquoise tesserae listed as tribute in the Codex Mendoza (folio 40r).

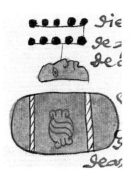

31 'Ten masks of rich blue stones' listed as tribute in the Codex Mendoza (folio 40r).

32 Samples of pyrite, turquoise and malachite (clockwise from top). The sample of turquoise is *c.* 7 cm across.

33 Palette of the colours of turquoise used on the mosaics.

34 Part of the immense Mount Chalchihuitl turquoise-mining pit at Los Cerillos, New Mexico.

35 Map indicating sites mentioned in the text and showing the main routes by which turquoise reached Mexico.

36 Turquoise vein at Old Hachita, New Mexico; the pocket-knife is *c.* 6cm long.

district of New Mexico (see fig. 34 and map, fig. 35).[3] Turquoise occurs naturally as rounded concretions (fig. 32) or as fine-grained veinlets (fig. 36). The colours available at Mount Chalchihuitl encompass the full range of green-blue hues observed on surviving mosaics.[4] Turquoise from different geological locations varies slightly in composition, and studies to chemically identify or 'fingerprint' each potential source have been undertaken.[5] The results indicate that much of the turquoise used for the Mexican mosaics was obtained from Los Cerrillos, perhaps supplemented by material of lesser quality from other sources.[6] Sahagún has much to say about the qualities and procurement of mined turquoise and other minerals (fig. 37):

'And how is it with the turquoise? It comes out of a mine. From within it is removed: the fine turquoise, the even, the smoked; and that called turquoise or ruby; and then the amber, the rock crystal, the obsidian; and then the flint, the mirror stone, the jet, the bloodstone. All are from mines.'[7]

He describes fine turquoise as that which has no inclusions or surface imperfections and is pale in colour;[8] other turquoise is 'a little dark surfaced'. Interestingly, the latter 'is required for use in adorning; it is just set on, glued on, for which there is gluing of the surface', perhaps a reference to mosaic working?

Turquoise procurement (fig. 35) appears to have been dominated by inland markets and the Mixtec polities of the Pacific coast lying between

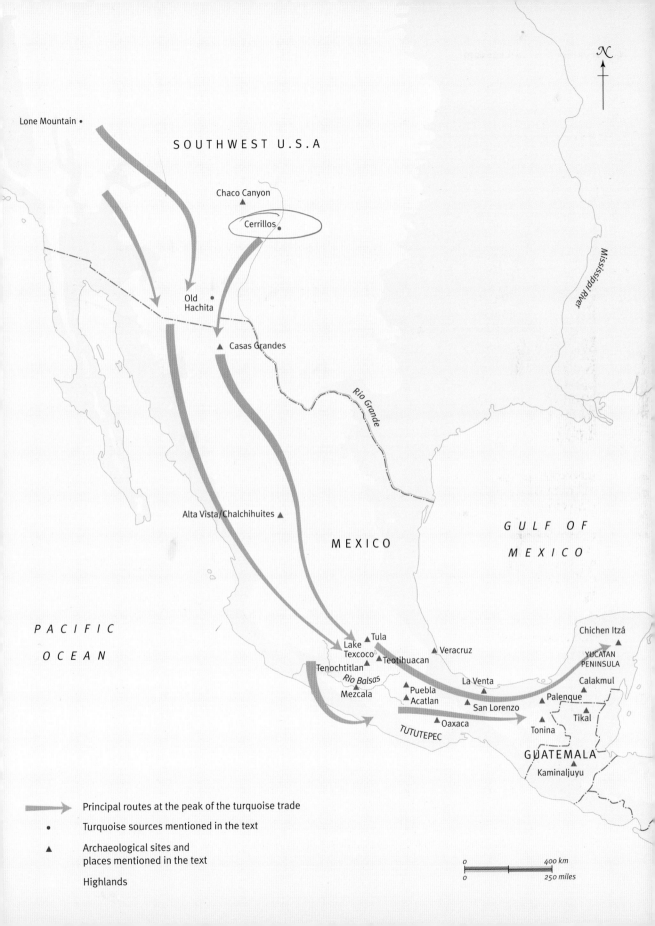

N

Lone Mountain •

SOUTHWEST U.S.A

Chaco Canyon ▲

Cerrillos •

Old
Hachita •

Casas Grandes ▲

Rio Grande

Mississippi River

Alta Vista/Chalchihuites ▲

MEXICO

GULF OF
MEXICO

PACIFIC

OCEAN

Tula ▲
Lake
Texcoco
Teotihuacan ▲
Tenochtitlan ▲
Rio Balsas
Puebla ▲
Mezcala ▲
Acatlan ▲

Veracruz ▲

La Venta ▲

San Lorenzo ▲

Oaxaca ▲

TUTUTEPEC

Tonina ▲

Chichen Itzá
▲
YUCATAN
PENINSULA

Calakmul ▲

Palenque ▲

Tikal ▲

GUATEMALA

Kaminaljuyu ▲

Principal routes at the peak of the turquoise trade

• Turquoise sources mentioned in the text

▲ Archaeological sites and
places mentioned in the text

Highlands

0   400 km

0   250 miles

37 Sahagún's depiction of turquoise deposits (Bk. 11, ill. 767).

Acatlan and Tututepec. It was mined and fashioned into tesserae on Mesoamerica's northern frontier, where it was used in exchange for hides, feathers and other perishable commodities.[9] The tesserae were transported over huge distances into west Mexico by Chichimec entrepreneurs. The Mixtecs probably imported it by dealing with west Mexican middlemen, possibly bringing it in through the Rio Balsas drainage area by overland trails, and also by sea along the Pacific coast.[10] The Mixtecs seem to have been instrumental in channelling trade in turquoise and redistributing the precious commodity throughout much of the rest of Mesoamerica. The Mixtec codices show finely crafted gold, silver, jade and turquoise jewels, plus ornaments of quetzal and macaw feathers, being offered to reward loyal subjects for their services and to exchange with alliance partners for other goods and favours.

MALACHITE When darker shades of green were required as elements of the designs, malachite was used. This is a carbonate mineral, again coloured by copper. Malachite, like turquoise, is rarely found as well-formed crystals. Instead, it is usually fine grained and often distinctly banded (fig. 32), a feature that can be seen on several of the mosaics.

PYRITE Sometimes called 'fool's gold', because of its shiny golden appearance (fig. 32), pyrite, an iron sulphide mineral, was shaped and polished as orbs for use as eyes on several of the mosaics. Pyrite can tarnish, taking on a dark metallic lustre, and was probably chosen, at least in part, for this quality. Occasionally pieces of pyrite were used among other tesserae to form different design elements.

FLINT Flint (*tecpatl* in Náhuatl) is hard and tough, being a very fine-grained (cryptocrystalline) variety of quartz; it is similar to chert and the two terms are often used interchangeably, although some authorities restrict the use of the term 'flint' to material occurring as nodules in chalk. Flint was used for the blade of the turquoise mosaic knife (see ch. 3).

LIGNITE OR JET These are forms of coal. According to Sahagún, jet (*teutetl*) 'is precious, rare like the special attribute of a god. It is black, very black, completely black … perfect in its blackness'.[11] Lignite was used on the mosaic mask of the god Tezcatlipoca (see fig. 102), to form the three dramatic horizontal bands that run across the face, contrasting sharply with alternating bands of blue turquoise.

GOLD   Known as *teocuitlatl* in Náhuatl, the 'excrement of the sun',[12] gold was, accord-ing to Sahagún, 'wonderful, yellow, good, fine, precious'.[13] Gold is widely distributed as the native element, with deposits in many parts of modern Mexico, including the central region.[14] In pre-Hispanic times it was obtained by mining and panning,[15] and many gold items are listed as tribute in the Codex Mendoza, including beads, discs and bowls of fine gold-dust.[16] It is rather sparingly used on the mosaics; the remains of gold foil are only readily visible on the mosaic shield, although microscopic traces survive on several others. In all cases the foil must have served to highlight the areas of design where it was used, as described by Sahagún: 'I hammer the gold leaf. I gild something…. Thus I make things beautiful; thus I make things give off rays.'[17] The very modest use of gold on the mosaics described here, and indeed on other surviving examples, is not necessarily typical for turquoise mosaic art. Many of the mosaics that are listed in the sixteenth-century inventories seem to feature gold to a much greater extent,[18] perhaps rendering them more vulnerable to break up and loss after their arrival in Europe.

PIGMENTS   In the places where the wooden surfaces were not covered by mosaic they were often painted. In some cases the paint is on very visible areas of the objects and would have contributed to the overall dramatic decorative effect. Other painted areas, however, must have been concealed during use – for example the inside of the helmet – and their presence is another example of the high quality of finish on the objects. Resins were also coloured with pigments although this practice was restricted to areas where the resin was intended to be visible. The naturally occurring mineral pigments that have been identified on the British Museum mosaics are bright red cinnabar (mercury sulphide), hematite (red iron oxide) and red ochre (hematite with other iron oxides, clay and silica). These are natural materials that could have been obtained from surface deposits or by mining. In contrast, Maya blue, the bright blue pigment present on the helmet, would have been manufactured by combining the organic dye indigo (from *Indigofera* sp.) with fine palygorskite clay.[19] Maya blue was widely used in Mesoamerica, possibly until the twentieth century, and has exceptional durability on account of the complex way in which the indigo and the clay are combined.[20]

GEMSTONES   Among the mosaics in the British Museum, the use of gems such as rubies, emeralds and garnets was restricted to the animal head (see fig. 126). These gems will be described more fully when the history of this mosaic is discussed in chapter 3.

SHELL   Teeth and fangs were fashioned with white shell, while a variety of orange, yellow, salmon-pink, rose-pink and red-coloured shells were used for the decorative, geometric and symbolic motifs (fig. 38). Many different species of marine (and fresh-water) shells have been carved and decorated to form a wide range of geometric,

(a)

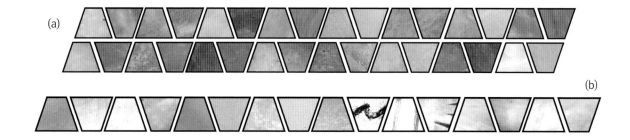

(b)

38 Palettes of (a) coloured shells and (b) the mother-of-pearl shell used on the mosaics.

39 *Spondylus princeps* bivalve shell, *c.*125 mm wide.

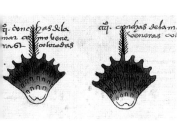

40 *Spondylus* shells in the Codex Mendoza (folio 38r).

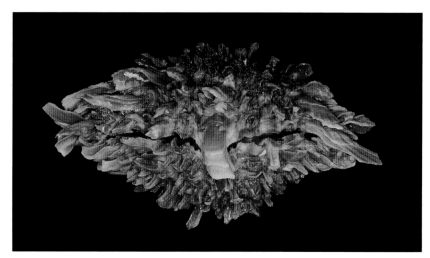

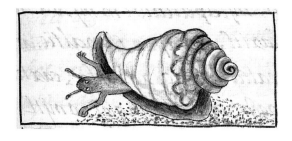

41 *Strombus gigas* (conch), as illustrated by Sahagún (Bk 11, ill.198).

anthropomorphic and zoomorphic artefacts. Three species in particular were identified during the examination of the mosaics: *Spondylus* species – commonly known as the thorny oyster – the pearl oyster *Pinctada mazatlantica* and the large conch shells of the *Strombus* genus. Fresh specimens of *Spondylus princeps* (thorny oyster; figs 39, 40) are excellent sources of deep red shell. *Spondylus* shells, however, can be very variable in colour: some specimens yield bright orange, purplish-red, dark to light salmon-pinks and vivid coral-coloured tones, while others may be predominantly white, with minimal red or orange areas. When *Spondylus* shell is cut from weathered or dead specimens, the dark red, coral red and bright orange typical of the live shell commonly fade to salmon pinks, reddish-pink, reddish-purple and light orange shades. The shell tesserae display this broad palette of red, salmon-pink, reddish-purple and orange tones, which would have come from both live and dead shells. Several species within the *Strombus* (conch) genus also yield a range of red, orange and pink hues, which exhibit a faded colour spectrum on weathering. The main species of conch that are of importance in the context of the turquoise mosaics are *Strombus gigas* (queen conch; fig. 41) and *S. galeatus* (Cortés conch), which offer white, pink, yellow and orange shell.

Colour was an important consideration in the choice of shell, and contrasting colours were often combined to achieve striking effects, as in the gaping mouth of the double-headed serpent mosaic (fig. 42; see p.54). Here, the bright reddish-pink *Spondylus princeps* shell of the gums contrasts vividly with the white *Strombus* shell teeth and the blue of the turquoise. Mother-of-pearl shell, probably from *Pinctada mazatlantica* (pearl oyster; see for example figs 61, 62), was also used, especially for eyes and for incised segments.

Spondylus princeps (fig. 39) and *Spondylus calcifer* favour warm-water habitats in the Gulf of Mexico and the Caribbean, and on the Pacific coast from Ecuador to the Gulf of

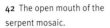
42 The open mouth of the serpent mosaic.

California. Part of the 'value' of *Spondylus princeps*, in particular, may be linked to the difficulty of diving for these bivalves, often at depths of twenty-five to sixty metres or more. *Strombus* species have a wide geographical range in the tropical and temperate coastal waters of both the Atlantic and the Caribbean. The populations of *Pinctada mazatlantica* and the smaller *Pinctada imbricata* in the Gulf of California, or 'Sea of Cortés, on

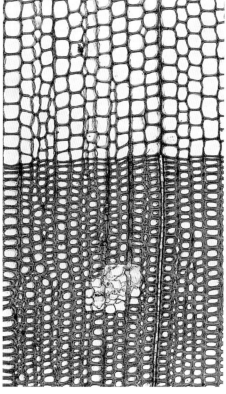

43 Illustration from Sahagún (Bk 1, ill. 34), showing wood working.

44 The transverse view of the characteristic cellular structure of the softwood *Pinus* sp. seen at high magnification.

45 Pine trees illustrated by Sahagún (Bk 11, ill. 377).

Mexico's Pacific coast, have been significant since pre-Columbian times, in terms of both the bivalves themselves and the pearls they may have yielded. The trading of shells from these areas would have involved transport over distances of several hundred kilometres.[21]

WOOD AND FIBRE The most popular choice of wood for the mosaics was the hardwood *Cedrela odorata*, Mexican cedar (see fig. 27), which has a wide distribution in the New World in moist and seasonally dry subtropical or tropical forests. This aromatic, reddish-brown wood is much in demand even today, as it is naturally insect-resistant, durable and easily worked. Traditionally, it has been used for boxes, fine furniture and other carved artefacts. For some of the turquoise mosaic artefacts the wood was carved to produce curved shapes, which were then modified to create the three-dimensional 'models' onto which the tesserae were placed. In some instances the wood was pierced or chiselled to make holes for decorative or functional purposes. Sahágun says the carpenter 'works carefully, skillfully; he sculptures in wood, carves it, smooths the surface, fits the wood, saws it, lashes it, forms tenons, forms recesses'[22] (fig. 43).

A softwood, *Pinus* sp., pine (figs. 44, 45), was used for the shield, but because many pines are anatomically very similar, it was not possible to identify the particular species of pine. Pine species can be found across a wide range of ecological conditions in Mexico at altitudes of 800 to about 3,500 metres, although they do not occur in the Yucatán peninsula or on the coastal plains along the Pacific and the Gulf of Mexico. Most pines favour warm temperate or temperate climatic conditions, but some species

46 'Copal' resin from *Bursera* sp.

are found in subtropical zones and a couple in tropical and in cold temperate habitats. In order to hold the blade of the mosaic knife firmly in the wooden handle, the haft was bound tightly with cord made from the natural fibre (maguey) of the agave plant, which has a widespread local distribution. As well as being a source of fibre, it was used as a medicine and to make pulque, an alcoholic drink; even the barbs were useful – as needles.

RESINS The resins were used primarily as adhesives on the mosaics, but also decoratively as inlays, to create relief designs and, mixed with pigment, usually the red iron-oxide hematite, to contribute colour.

Pine resin is particularly common on the mosaics examined here. It is not possible to infer the species from the resin chemistry, but resin is collected from a range of pines,

47 *Copalquahuitl*, the 'copal' tree, as illustrated by Hernandez (1943: fig. 117).

48 *Bursera* tree.

including *Pinus oocarpa, P. pseudostrobus* and *P. leiophylla*, by the modern indigenous population, who use it as incense, medicine and adhesive.[23]

Sahagún refers to pine resin in Náhuatl as *ocotzotl* while using the name *oxitl* to describe unguents made from pine.[24] He also reports the association of *oxitl* with the fire god Xiuhtecuhtli,[25] and because of this, the use of heat in its production has sometimes been inferred, and reference then made to the distillation of turpentine[26] or perhaps the production of pitch. Refining or modification of pine resin by heat was clearly common practice, as Sahagún indicates that 'cooked', 'uncooked' and 'boiled' pine resin were available in the marketplace.[27] If *oxitl* was a turpentine or pitch it was not used on the mosaics, for these pine resins show no chemical evidence for extensive heating or distillation.

Copalli was the Náhuatl word for resin and a wide range of resins are still known throughout Mesoamerica as 'copal' (fig. 46). The term is rather misleading as true copal resins come from resin-producing trees of the Fabaceae (Leguminosae) family, while the

Mesoamerican 'copals' are normally referred to as 'elemi' elsewhere and come from very different trees of the Bursaraceae family.[28] The Aztecs named these trees after the resin they produced, for example *copalquahuitl* ('copal' tree) and *tecopalquahuitl pitzahoac* (narrow-leaved 'copal' tree). Francisco Hernández described (1571–7) at least sixteen such varieties, and noted the uses of the resins.[29] Some of them he illustrated (for example fig. 47) and these are mostly thought to be various types of *Bursera* (fig. 48), of which there are at least a hundred species in Mexico; most grow in warm dry areas.[30] The resins of many of these trees are still extracted for traditional uses by local communities; *B. excelsa*, *B. bipinnata* and *B. tomentosa* provide incense while *B. simaruba* is used as a domestic medicine and as an adhesive.[31] *Bursera* resins were identified on two of the mosaics (the serpent and the helmet), sometimes mixed with pine resin. *Protium copal*, also of the Burseraceae family, yields another 'copal' resin and was cultivated by the ancient Maya for incense.[32] It is still used as incense in Mesoamerica, as well as medicinally. Nowadays it is only harvested from the wild, but the resin must have been exploited extensively in the past, though perhaps more as incense than adhesive; it occurs on only one of the mosaics (the knife).

All of the resins can be sourced from trees indigenous to Mexico. The extensive use of pine resin on these objects is interesting but whether it is typical for Mixtec-Aztec mosaics is difficult to judge. Although Sahagún mentions the gluing of mosaics,[33] the kind of adhesive used is not clear and neither pine nor 'copal' is mentioned specifically. However, pine and 'copal' resin have been suggested as the adhesives on other mosaics that have been closely examined in the past.[34] Pine and Burseraceae trees tend to occupy rather different vegetational niches, so it is possible that the use of pine resin on some objects and 'copal' resins on others reflects the local availability of the materials, though both would have been readily available in the marketplace.[35] Other plant-derived 'glues' have also been identified from the mosaics; for example, a mixture of charcoal and chia seed oil called *chaute* has been identified on Postclassic mosaic fragments from Oaxaca.[36] A rather different adhesive material, a gritty cement, has been described from other mosaics.[37]

BEESWAX Beeswax has been used the world over since the earliest times as an adhesive, sealant and lamp fuel. Bees were kept for their honey in pre-Hispanic times and pictures of bees and beekeeping feature in the codices. The wax would have been a useful by-product: Sahagún describes the 'lost-wax' casting of metals,[38] although its employment for lighting was introduced by the Spanish, as Martyr observes: 'Instead of candles and torches they burn pine resin.… Neither do they make any use of wax, although they have both wax and honey, which they have only learned to use since our arrival'.[39] Certainly beeswax was applied only sparingly on the mosaics, possibly as a filler or putty, and also to create moulded decoration.

49 A lapidary passes on his skills to his son (Codex Mendoza, folio 70r).

50 Lapidary at work (Sahagún Bk 9, ill. 68).

Construction of the mosaics

Skilled lapidaries in service to the Aztec royal court and nobility were charged with the task of working stone into finely carved and decorated artefacts. These stoneworkers were organized into guilds and their specialist skills were passed down from generation to generation by word of mouth and example, perhaps within family groups (fig. 49). Whether the lapidaries who made the turquoise mosaics were Aztecs is, however, debatable. Certainly there is evidence that the mosaics were, in fact, made by Mixtec craftsmen,[40] who may or may not have been directly employed by the Aztecs.

The lapidaries were highly regarded by the Aztec rulers: indeed, Durán records how Motecuhzoma (ruled 1502–20) went to war with the provinces of Quetzaltepec and Tototepec over access to materials they needed for stone polishing.[41] Sahagún describes how the turquoise was ground and polished: 'fine turquoise is not very hard. With just a little sand it is polished; with it, it is embellished. And also, it may be given brilliance, radiance, [with] another tool called a turquoise-burnisher.'[42]

In the same passage he refers also to the polishing of 'round turquoise', for which no hard abrasive was needed; instead 'it is rubbed with a piece of fine cane, so that it may give forth rays of light, may glisten'.[43] Sahagún notes that the lapidary is well taught, and informed in his art; he can judge good quality stones and is able to abrade and polish them to a fine shiny finish[44] (fig. 50). He continues, recording that the lapidary is a creator of 'works of skill', bringing together the stones with glue to make the mosaics, although this is not illustrated.

The polishing marks left by the lapidary are remarkably clear when viewed under the microscope (fig. 51). The grinding marks often lie in markedly different directions on adjacent tesserae, showing that they must have been ground smooth separately before they were set in place. Close observation has also shown that some of the tesserae were carefully prepared with bevelled edges – a feature noted in studies of turquoise working at sites such as Alta Vista.[45] This enabled closer fitting of the tesserae over the curved surfaces of the objects.

Shells of *Spondylus*, *Strombus* and *Pinctada* may have been selected as live specimens for

51 Photomicrograph of tesserae showing grinding marks. The large tesserae are *c.* 5mm across

52 Illustration showing shell working (Sahagún Bk11, ill. 788).

subsequent working, but some of the tesserae appear to have been made from weathered or 'dead' shells from beach deposits. A range of tools would have been needed to prepare and work these very different types of shell.[46] 'Dead' conch shells washed up on beaches might have already been fragmented into manageable pieces by wave action, but a heavy-duty implement, such as a stone hammer, would have been required to break up the dense shell of a live conch. In the case of *Spondylus*, a small stone tool may have been used to remove the spines and hinges of the shell and to grind smooth the radial bands on each valve. The more fragile *Pinctada* bivalve shell would have needed careful cutting and shaping with a sharp-edged obsidian or flint blade.

The fragments of *Spondylus*, *Strombus* and *Pinctada* were probably then marked out for precise cutting and shaping into tesserae using a lithic (stone) point or awl. The actual cutting (fig. 52) could have been carried out effectively with an angled lithic tool or by weaving away a cut made to an edge of the shell and working it with cord or fibres, perhaps also with the aid of a loose abrasive, such as fine quartz. Some of the shell tesserae have incised surface decoration; notable examples are the engraved *Pinctada* mother-of-pearl segments on the jaguar (see p.78). This effect could have been achieved with a sharp lithic blade or angled point, after the main shaping and polishing phase. An awl or hand-held rotary drill was used to perforate some of the shell pieces that represent eyes and ear ornaments.

Apart from the human skull mosaic (fig. 102), the prepared tesserae were applied to wood, which was shaped to the required form, and, if appropriate, fine details were carved into its surface, as can be seen on the knife handle shown in fig. 53. In the Florentine Codex Sahagún depicts typical woodworking tools. These were presumably in use at the time of the Spanish Conquest but may also be representative of tree-felling and carpentry tools from earlier periods. One of the illustrations shows a tree being cut down and trimmed with a hafted chisel-like axe (see fig. 43). In another a wooden figurine is being carved with a similar chisel-like artefact struck with a separate wooden mallet. Other drawings show hafted adzes being used to hollow out (charred?) wood to form a canoe. These woodworking and carpentry practices could have been carried out with just stone or shell tools; it is very doubtful whether metal artefacts were widely available at the time for such purposes. There is no doubting, however, the fine carpentry skills and intimate knowledge of wood properties exhibited by the woodworkers in the crafting of the turquoise mosaics. Traces of carpentry tool-marks can be seen clearly on the back of the 'warty' mask in fig. 65, on the reverse of the double-headed serpent in fig. 80 and on the helmet (fig. 73d); and they testify to the fine control exercised by the carpenters.

The tesserae were held in place using pine or 'copal' resin (fig. 54). In some cases pine and 'copal' resins were mixed together; it is unclear whether this was intended to modify their properties or was an economic choice based on the materials available. Fresh Burseraceae resins are fragrant, pale yellow in colour and oily, with a consistency rather like crystallized honey. They have sometimes been added to varnishes to toughen them and reduce their brittleness, and their malleability when fresh could have improved the working properties of the pine resin. In addition, they are slow-drying, which may have been an advantage for the intricate mosaic work.[47] The malleability of the resin would have allowed tesserae of variable thickness to be pressed into the resin layer to different depths, maintaining an overall smooth surface

53 Knife, with carved but undecorated wooden handle; the flint blade is ancient but was added in modern times (h 7 x w 5 x l 31 cm).

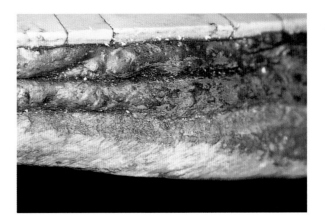

54 Photomicrograph from the turquoise mosaic mask of Xiuhtecuhtli or Nanahuatzh showing layers of resin between the wood and the tesserae; note the extremely precise positioning of the tesserae and their bevelled edges.

on the finished mosaic. Sometimes, however, 'copal' resin is found in one place on an object, while a 'copal'/pine mixture has been applied elsewhere on the same object. This perhaps indicates that the remaining 'copal' resin was merely supplemented by mixing it with the pine, rather than selected for specific properties. Nevertheless, there are cases where it is clear that the craftsmen were using mixtures to modify the properties of the materials to obtain the best result. For example, the moulded and gilded relief on the serpent mask (see fig. 68) was formed from a mixture of beeswax and pine resin: the beeswax would have taken to a mould more easily than sticky resin, while the addition of resin would have improved the adhesion of the gold foil.

It is possible that colour played a part in the selection of the resins. For example, the *Protium* 'copal' resin on the knife hafting may have been chosen for its pale colour, and the colour of pigment in the red resins shows up more brightly where mixed with the pale *Bursera* 'copal' resin on the serpent than with the darker pine resin on the serpent mask.

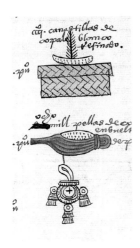

55 Refined and unrefined copal resin, listed as tribute in the Codex Mendoza (folio 36r).

56 'They seem to the naked eye to be one single stone'. The large tessera is *c.* 1 cm across. Detail from the turquoise mosaic serpent mask of Tlaloc.

It is impossible to tell whether the resins were applied in a freshly tapped, sticky state or as a melted solid because the gentle heating required to melt them does not leave any lasting evidence in the chemical composition. 'Copal' resins clearly underwent some kind of refining process for use in incense, as both refined and unrefined 'copal' are listed as tribute in the Codex Mendoza (fig. 55).[48] Whichever is the case, the craftsman's control on the materials was exceptional, with the result that the tesserae are fitted 'so artistically and perfectly joined together that it is impossible to detect their lines of junction with the fingernail. They seem to the naked eye to be one single stone'[49] (fig. 56).

The Turquoise Mosaics in the British Museum Collections

The turquoise mosaics in the British Museum collections are renowned for their high quality and, in many cases, very complete state, and they have been described and illustrated many times.[1] Now, through the scientific work underpinning this book, more detailed descriptions than ever before can be presented with 'close-up' views of the mosaics in microscope and radiographic images. Comparisons are drawn with examples from other collections but these are by no means exhaustive and the main focus is on the mosaics that have been examined in detail.

The masks

Masks feature in the sacred and secular practices of past and present societies around the world serving both to reveal and conceal. Masks hide the real identity of the wearer in order to project an alternative persona. In Mesoamerica masks were often used to signal the threshold between visible reality and the invisible world of ancestor spirits and deities. Masks were worn by priests to personify ancestors and gods in ritual enactments that rendered their deeds and activities visible and intelligible for an earthly audience. Martyr reports that masks were 'placed upon the faces of the gods, whenever the sovereign is ill, not to be removed until he either recovers or dies.'[2] Funerary masks

57 Mortuary bundle of a Mixtec lord wearing a mask. Codex Zouche-Nuttall, p. 82.

(fig. 57) were used to communicate the divine attributes and immortality of deceased rulers. The role they played in funerary practice is described by Ixtlilxochitl,[3] who records the burial rites for Tezozomoc, the King of Azcapotazalco, an Aztec town in the basin of Mexico:

'they washed the body well … And then they dressed it in the royal robes and the jewels of gold and precious stones … they put it on a mat in a seated position, and placed a very life-like turquoise mask on the face, made according to the features of the dead man.'[4]

The Aztecs valued the artefacts of their predecessors and are known to have found and reused Teotihuacán and Olmec stone masks.[5] Painted designs or carved features were sometimes added before they were placed in ritual offerings. Mezcala (*c.* 500–200 BC) masks were transformed into Aztec gods by the addition of the painted faces of Xiuhtecuhtli or Tlaloc; there is a single example of a Teotihuacán stone mask embellished at some point in its history by the application of a mosaic design.[6]

58 Wooden mask with turquoise decoration, found in a cave in the Tehuacan region of Puebla, *c.* 1500 (h 15.5 x w 15 cm).

Masks in stone, clay and wood were made for use in temple rituals. Most of the wooden masks that survive were originally decorated with turquoise.[7] These were probably acquired by the Aztec rulers of Tenochtitlán as part of the tribute paid by subject populations; ten masks of rich blue stones (see fig. 31) are listed in the Codex Mendoza. A cache of such masks was discovered early in the twentieth century in a dry cave in the state of Puebla, to the southeast of Tenochtitlán, and another group was recovered in 1986 from a similar location.[8] Only one of these masks retains a significant proportion of its turquoise and, interestingly, also features onyx as inlay over the right eye socket and as teeth in the mouth (fig. 58). The mosaic on this Puebla mask comprises relatively large, polygonal tesserae of green turquoise, apparently set in a 'sea' of minute blue tesserae[9] – rather different to the mosaic technique used on the two masks now in the British Museum.

The mask in fig. 59 may represent Xiuhtecuhtli, the Central Mexican god of fire. The name 'Xiuhtecuhtli' also means Turquoise Lord, and this god is shown in the codices adorned with turquoise.[10] One of the emblems of Xiuhtecuhtli is the butterfly, and it has been suggested that there is a stylized image of a 'butterfly' on the mask – the wings picked out in more intense blue turquoise on the two cheeks.[11] However, the design on the mosaic mask is elusive, and detailed examination, including electronic re-processing of colour images and careful re-drawings, indicates that this is at best a subjective impression. There are other turquoise masks that show similar concentrated areas of high colour on the cheeks and forehead.[12]

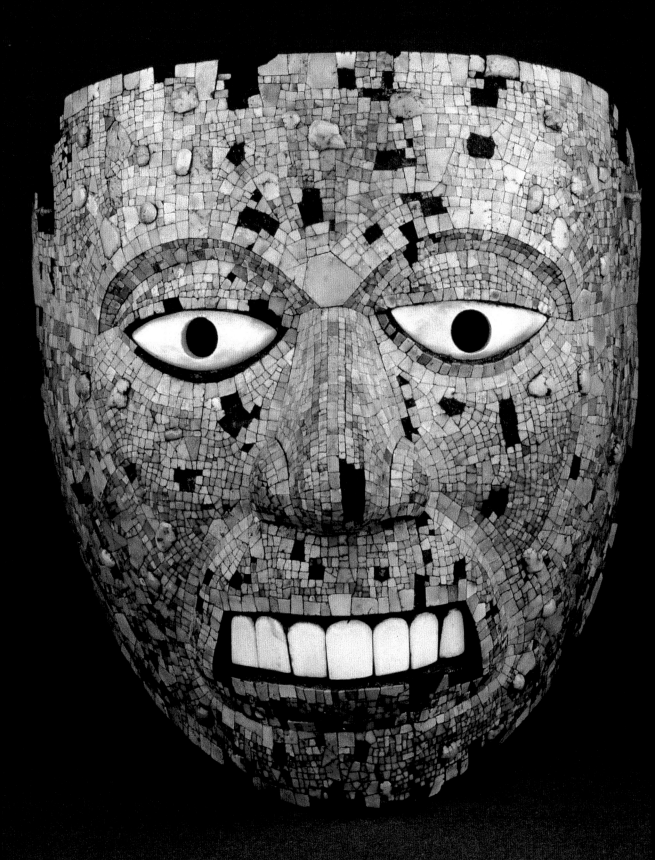

59 Turquoise mosaic mask of Xiuhtecuhtli or Nanahuatzh.

60 Turquoise 'wart'.

61 *Pinctada* mother-of-pearl eye.

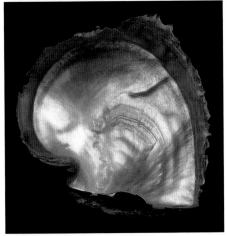

62 *Pinctada* mother-of-pearl shell.

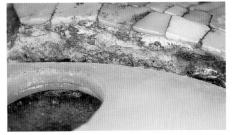

63 Detail showing the application of gold in the eye.

A feature of this mask is the use of raised turquoise cabochons, producing the effect of 'warts'. These 'warts', clearly visible all over the face, are formed from smooth, shiny nodules of turquoise applied so that they overlap the surrounding turquoise tesserae (fig. 60). Because of the 'warts', it has been proposed that this mask may in fact represent Nanahuatzh, who was a small leprous god with boils on his face who cast himself into a great fire at the time of the creation, only to rise from the fire to become the sun (Tonatiuh).[13]

The elliptical eyes (fig. 61) that give the mask an arresting presence are made from carved pieces of mother-of-pearl shell (*Pinctada mazatlantica*) (fig. 62), each with a circular central hole. A similar style of eye occurs on other mosaics[14] and several comparable pairs of pierced shell ellipses excavated at Monte Albán have been interpreted as the remains of mosaic masks.[15] The eyelids were gilded (fig. 63) and examination by SEM has revealed that the gold was applied as a thin foil about one hundredth of a millimetre thick.[16]

The partly open mouth has seven 'teeth', all in the 'upper jaw' made from white conch shell, either *Strombus gigas* or *S. galeatus* (fig. 64). Most of these are thought to be original features of the mask. However, close examination reveals that two of the teeth are made from a modern composite.[17] It is not known when these teeth were replaced; seven are recorded as being present in 1895.[18]

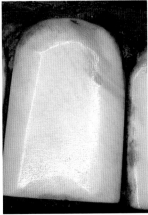

64 Tooth made from white *Strombus* shell.

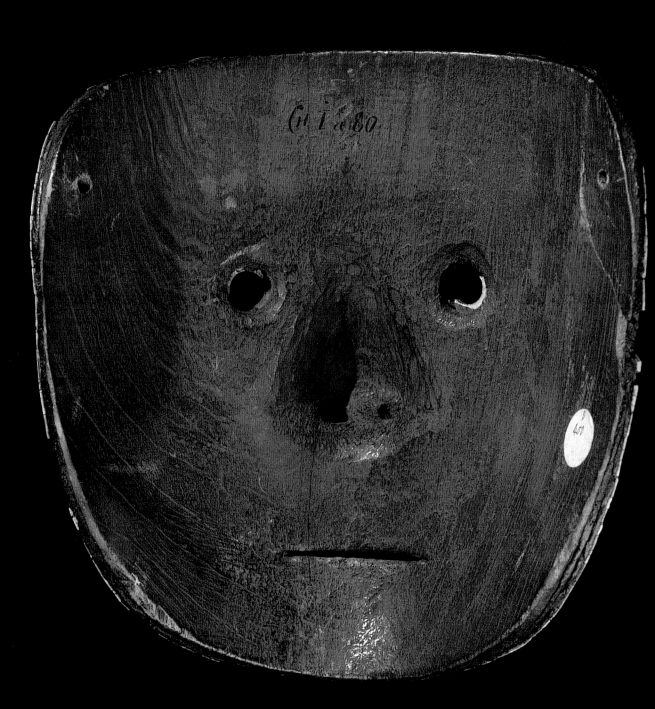

65 Reverse of the mask, showing red paint applied to the wood.

The mosaic design was laid over the surface of a single piece of *Cedrela odorata* wood using pine resin. The arrangement of the mosaic over the rounded nose and flaring nostrils and delineating the brow ridges is comparable to the mosaic technique on a number of other mosaic masks.[19] The wood was carved to produce a curve and the underlying contours of the face. The reverse of the mask is coloured with red pigment (fig. 65) identified as cinnabar; this pigment was used on other Aztec objects including a stone rattlesnake (fig. 66), where it was applied in the mouth and also to form bright red spots on the underside of the body.

Suspension holes at the temples, each originally decorated by a plate of mother-of-pearl shell (fig. 67), indicate that the mask was intended to be worn, or perhaps tied to another object. If the mask was worn over the face, the apertures in the shell eye inserts would have allowed some vision for the wearer, although this style of eyes can be pierced even when they are purely decorative, as on the serpent's head on the Mixtec mask in the collections of L' Pigorini, Rome.[20] The mask may well have been worn by priests to impersonate a god in the enactment of scenes from creation myth cycles and to recount the deeds of culture heroes.[21]

The design of the mask shown in fig. 68 is strikingly different, being formed from two intertwined serpents of blue and green turquoise. At some time the mask was damaged

66 Stone snake with applied bright red cinnabar pigment (h 36, diam. 53 cm).

67 *Pinctada* mother-of-pearl plates used to finish the suspension hole.

OVERLEAF
68 Serpent mask of Tlaloc.

69 Radiograph of the serpent mask; note the bright white pegs used to make repairs to the mask.

and evidence of repair can be seen in the radiograph (fig. 69). The mask has been associated with the Feathered Serpent, Quetzalcoatl, mainly because of the plumes that hang down from the tails of the two serpents.[22] However, the way in which the serpents encircle the eyes creating the effect of 'goggles' is a feature typically associated with depictions of the rain god Tlaloc (fig. 70).

The very three-dimensional, sculptured surface of this mask was achieved by shaping, carving and perforating the single piece of *Cedrela odorata* wood. In addition to the perforations that are used to accentuate the design there is a suspension hole in each temple, suggesting that this mask could have been worn. The interior of the wooden surface was painted red, using red ochre. The different hues of turquoise were used to maximize the impact of the design of the intertwined serpents, one serpent worked in predominantly blue colours, the other in greener shades. The size and shape of the tesserae on this mask are quite variable, possibly indicating that some of the turquoise was recycled. Particularly prominent are the two large tesserae above the eyes, one of which is engraved (fig. 71a). Engraved tesserae are seen on other mosaics, for example on the figure of Tlaloc (fig. 72);[23] they were also used on the mosaic disc now in Vienna (fig. 93) and on the disc excavated in 1994 at the Templo Mayor of Tenochtitlan in Mexico City (see description on p.61).

Above the eyes of the mask are the rattles of the two snakes (fig. 71b); these were moulded from resin that has a more matt appearance than the pine resin used to attach the tesserae. Parts of the interior surface of the mask are coated with the same dull resin, identified as a mixture of pine resin and beeswax. The rattles were not covered by mosaic, but the presence of minute flecks of gold suggests that they were gilded. Pine resin coloured red with hematite (fig. 71c) was used to attach the conch shell teeth, four of which remain. Impressions in the resin indicate that there were originally seven teeth.

70 Representation of Tlaloc, on a ceramic pot (h 35 x w 35 x d 31.5 cm).

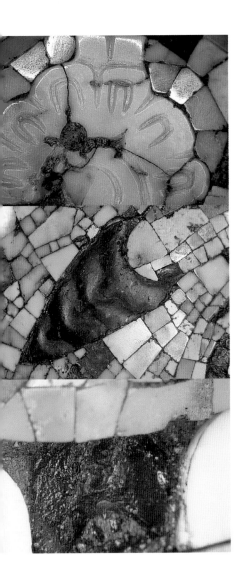

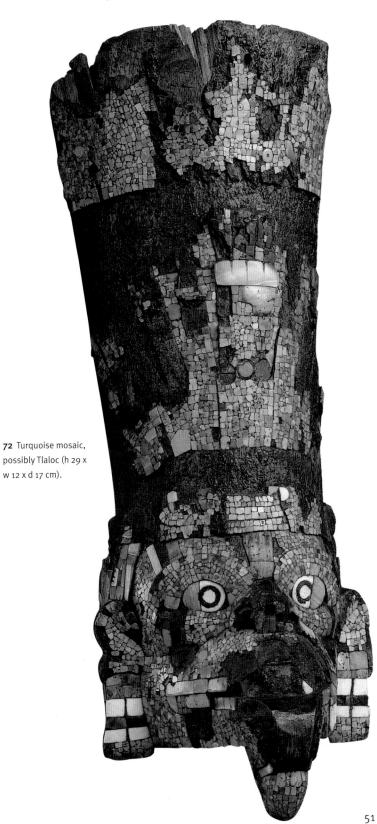

72 Turquoise mosaic, possibly Tlaloc (h 29 x w 12 x d 17 cm).

71 Details from the serpent mask (fig. 68): **(a)** engraved tessera; **(b)** 'rattle' of snake, moulded from beeswax and resin and probably gilded originally; **(c)** red pigmented resin used for 'gums' and to affix the white *Strombus* shell teeth.

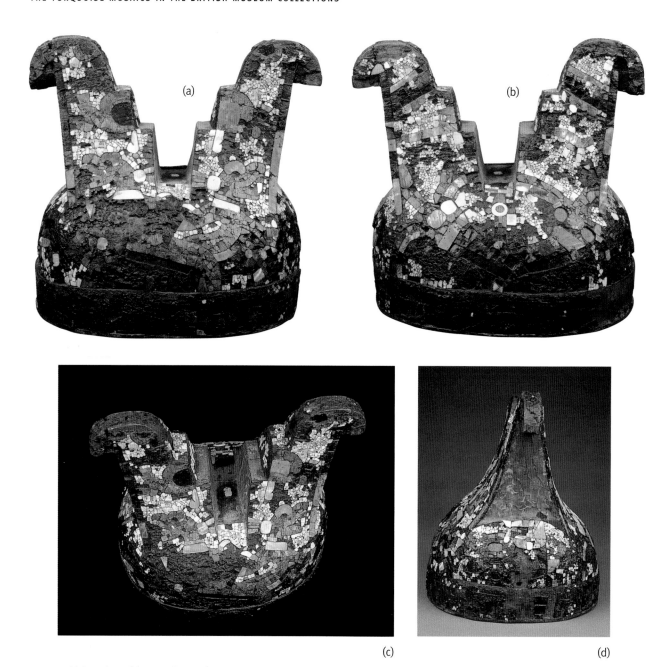

73 Various views of the turquoise mosaic
helmet: **(a&b)** from the side;
(c) from above; **(d)** 'end-on', showing the
undecorated surface of one of the 'beaks'
and tool marks on the bare wood.

The helmet

The helmet (fig. 73) is unique among the known turquoise mosaics from Mexico, although 'helmets of wood, some decorated with mosaic work' are listed in the inventories of artefacts sent back to Charles I of Spain (Emperor Charles V). It has not yet been possible to recognize comparable headpieces in the codices or on sculpture, perhaps because some components of the helmet are missing; helmets in the inventories, for example, are often described as having plumes of feathers.[24]

The helmet was carved from a single piece of *Cedrela odorata* wood. The interior was hollowed out so that it could be worn (fig. 75a). The orientation of the oval hollow suggests that the helmet was worn with the two 'beak-like' projections[25] at front and back, rather than on either side as the helmet is conventionally illustrated. The interior surface is coated with a rather dull-green-coloured paint; microscopical examination has revealed that the paint was originally bright turquoise blue (fig. 75b). The paint was coloured by indigo and gives a Raman spectrum identical with Maya Blue. Most of the exterior surface was decorated with mosaic, although much of this has been lost, exposing large areas of the mixture of pine and *Bursera* resins used to fix the tesserae in place. However, the outer faces of the two projections, and also the sides of the broad 'notch' on the top of the helmet, do not bear any traces of resin. It seems that these were never decorated with mosaic. Traces of red paint suggest that at least parts of these areas were painted, although they may have been largely concealed if there were feathers attached. The exposure of the bare wooden surface allows the marks of the tool used to shape the wood to be seen clearly (fig. 73d).

Large areas of tesserae have been lost and as a result parts of the mosaic design are difficult to discern; fig. 74 is intended to assist the perception and interpretation of the

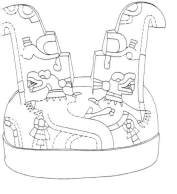

74 Diagram indicating a possible reconstruction of the original mosaic design on one side of the helmet (see fig. 73a).

75 (a) The hollowed out interior of the helmet, showing the green-blue paint; **(b)** detail of the paint, revealing the original bright blue colour.

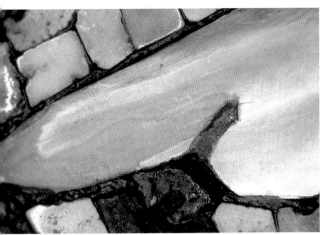

76 Some of the yellowish-coloured, mother-of-pearl shell used on the helmet.

77 Reddish-pink *Spondylus* shell and malachite on the 'crests' of the serpents.

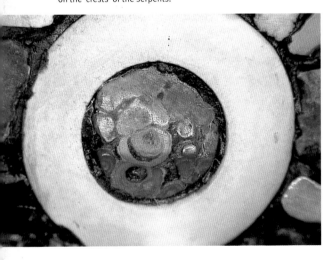

mosaic design. On one side of the helmet the heads of two outward-facing clawed serpents can be seen; these probably represent the Fire Serpent, Xiuhcoatl. Their main features were picked out in red *Spondylus* shell and dark green malachite. White mother-of-pearl shell was used for the large fang of one of the serpents, while the smaller teeth within the gaping jaws were indicated by sharp triangular pieces of rather pale-coloured turquoise. Distinctive yellowish-coloured mother-of-pearl shell (fig. 76), reddish-pink *Spondylus* shell and malachite (fig. 77) form the 'crests' on the heads of the serpents. It is not clear whether the bodies of the serpents extend onto the other side of the helmet, but two conical elements may represent quetzal-plume panaches, worn by the aristocracy.[26] White conch shell forms the circular surround to a polished fragment of dark green, nodular malachite on this side of the helmet (fig. 78).

The double-headed serpent

Serpent imagery pervades the religious iconography of Mesoamerica,[27] and the Feathered Serpent, Quetzalcoatl, was one of the most important deities. Because snakes shed their skins, they are associated with renewal and transformation in Aztec mythology,[28] and their sinuous movement has been likened to moving water and wind.[29]

The turquoise mosaic serpent (fig. 79) was carved from *Cedrela odorata* wood, which was skilfully shaped and then hollowed out at the back to give the serpent its U-shaped body (fig. 80). The reverse side was not decorated with any mosaic but traces of gold were found in several areas, perhaps indicating that the now bare

78 The white *Strombus* shell and dark green malachite motif on the helmet.

79 Turquoise mosaic double-headed serpent.

80 The reverse of the serpent.

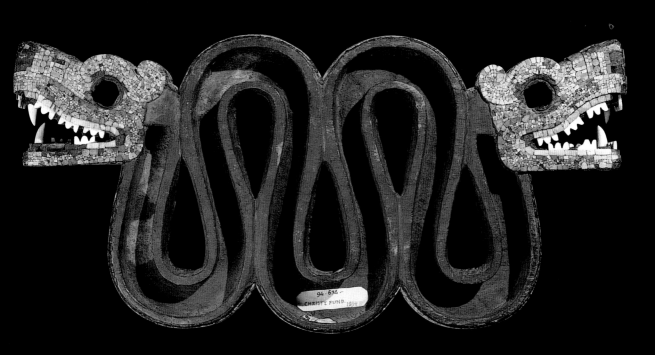

81 Detail of the serpent's head.

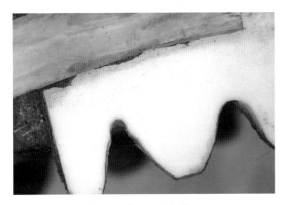

82 Teeth made of White *Strombus* conch shell.

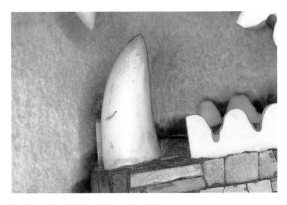

83 Fang of white *Strombus* conch shell.

wood was originally brightly gilded to form a dramatic contrast with the mosaic of the two heads, which were fully decorated on all surfaces.

The smoothly rounded body is covered in turquoise and it appears that darker and lighter coloured tesserae were selected to accentuate the play of light over the curves of the snake's body. The mixture of large tesserae along the line of the body, sometimes occurring as smoothly rounded cabochons, creates a tessellated surface that mimics the scaly patterned skin of the snake. In contrast to the smoothly curving profile of the snake's body, the heads are more planar, with sharp changes of level used to define the jaws and also the 'eyebrows' (fig. 81). The edges of these features are emphasized by meticulous alignment of tesserae. Within the gaping mouths, brightly coloured reddish-pink *Spondylus princeps* shell was used for the gums and white conch shell for the original teeth (fig. 82) and fangs (fig. 83).[30] On the reverse side the *Spondylus princeps* shell of the gums is orange in colour; it is possible that this colour was deliberately selected for the reverse, perhaps because it would be less visible. However, red *Spondylus* shell can weather to orange and, if this weathering took place *in situ* it may reflect the way in which the object was used or displayed at some time in its history. It is interesting to note that exactly the same combination of carved white conch shell teeth and reddish-pink *Spondylus* shell gums appears on a Maya jade mask from Mexico.[31] The style of the open mouths with fangs and jagged teeth is also strikingly similar to that of the jaguar head mosaic that was in Berlin.[32]

The shell tesserae used for the gums and teeth are held in place with resin from *Bursera* sp. (see ch. 2), which was coloured with hematite pigment so that the exposed resin between the teeth appears red. The same resin adhesive was applied elsewhere to fix the tesserae, but for this it was mixed with a small amount of pine resin and not pigmented.

84 Head (true left) of the double-headed serpent.

85 Detail of the nose, showing the use of reddish-pink *Spondylus* shell and bright blue turquoise.

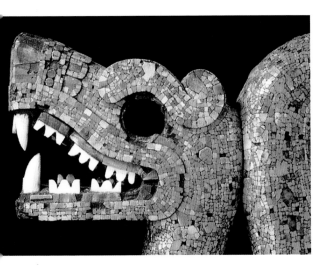

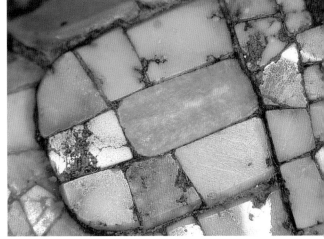

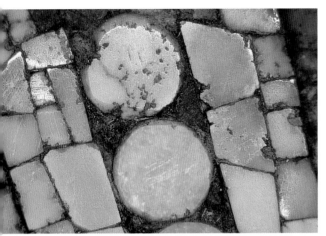

86 Circular pieces of mosaic on the nose.

87 Traces of beeswax around the (true right, front) eye socket.

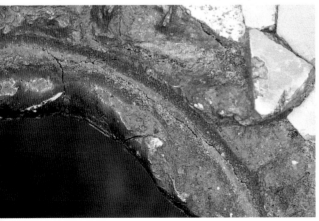

88 Traces of resin around the eye socket on the back of the (true right) head.

The most decorative areas of mosaic-work appear on the serpent heads; the striking red 'noses' were created from relatively large, triangular and lozenge-shaped tesserae of reddish-pink *Spondylus princeps* (fig. 84 and detail in fig. 85). *Spondylus* shell was also shaped into circular pieces and used with similar circular tesserae of deep blue turquoise to form a decorative band across each of the 'noses' (fig. 86). Unusually, the embedding resin around these circular tesserae seems to have been left exposed, setting the coloured band against a dark background.

The eye sockets are now hollow but traces of beeswax and resin remain around the rims (figs 87 and 88), suggesting that originally they would have been set with eyes, possibly polished orbs of pyrite similar to those used on the mosaic skull.

Particularly intriguing are the holes pierced through each of the lower jaws (fig. 89). The outline of each of these holes is clearly defined by four larger tesserae, and there is little doubt that they are part of the original design. Perhaps the two heads were fitted with moveable tongues, rather like that in the animal head that is now in the Museum für Völkerkunde in Vienna.[33]

The way in which the double-headed serpent mosaic was used has always been a subject of debate; it could

89 One of the lower jaws showing the pierced hole.

have been worn as a pectoral, suspended by a cord threaded through the holes at the top of two of the loops in the body. Alternatively, the serpent may have been fixed to a staff or standard as an identifying emblem. The traces of gilding on the reverse and the total coverage of the heads with mosaic suggest that it may have been intended to be seen from behind at times.

The shield

Warfare was an important aspect of Aztec life. High-ranking warriors were identified by brightly coloured regalia, and in the codices they are shown carrying wooden shields decorated with feathers arranged to form military insignia (fig. 90). Shields adorned with featherwork were probably used for ritual purposes rather than for protection in active warfare and they were sometimes imitated in stone, even to the extent of detailed representation of the holding straps on the reverse.[34] Wooden turquoise mosaic shields, too, seem to have been intended for use in ceremonies rather than in battle, an interpretation reinforced by the association of mosaic shields with the god Paynal, who represented Huitzilopochtli (god of sun and war) when there was a procession.[35] In Sahagún's account Paynal is shown holding a mosaic shield (fig. 91). The 'anonymous conqueror', a companion of Cortés, observed of mosaic shields 'they are not of the kind borne in war, but only those used in the festivals and dances which they are accustomed to have.'[36]

The designs on most of the 150 shields listed in the inventories of items sent back by Cortés were worked in feathers, but twenty-five are said to have been covered with turquoise mosaic;[37] some of these may have had feathers as well as turquoise. Few mosaic examples survive, but two, those in the British Museum (fig. 92) and in the Naturhistorisches Museum, Vienna (fig. 93),[38] are thought to have been brought to Europe early in the sixteenth century. Eight further fragmented mosaic shields, found in a cave in the Puebla region, are now in the National Museum of the American Indian in Washington.[39] Some of these shields are perhaps more appropriately referred to as 'discs' because of their small size and uncertainty about their intended function. During the 1990s a turquoise mosaic disc was recovered by excavation in the Templo Mayor, Tenochtitlan. This is still undergoing conservation and interpretation (see page 61).

90 Jaguar warrior with shield (Sahagún, Bk 2, pl. 2, ill. 5).

Capitulo segundo.   fo. ibidem.

91 Paynal shown holding a mosaic shield (Sahagún, Bk 1, pl. 2, ill. 2).

92 Turquoise mosaic shield.

93 Turquoise mosaic shield
(diam. 70 cm).

The turquoise mosaic disc from Offering 99 at the Templo Mayor, Tenochtitlán (fig. 94), was discovered during the 1994 excavations in the precinct known as 'The House of the Ajarajas'. The offering was buried during the last phase of construction of the Templo Mayor (1502–20) in front of the stairway that leads up to the shrine dedicated to Huitzilopochtli.

Some of the mosaic fragments were found adhering to the mud and clay surrounding the offering, while others had moved and were dispersed. Because of this and the attendant risks posed by excavation *in situ*, three large intact blocks were removed with the aid of metal sheets and a protective fabric. These blocks were then carefully excavated in the restoration laboratory of the Templo Mayor Museum, where some 15,000 fragments were recovered, cleaned and consolidated. The X-ray diffraction analysis of a representative sample enabled turquoise, malachite and calcite to be identified as the principal components.

The reconstruction of the mosaic was based on the position of the different pieces and the possibility of matching their bevelled edges. In this way it was possible to deduce that it was circular in form with an overall diameter of 28 cm. A darker central area is 8.5 cm in diameter, surrounded by a narrow band (1.5 cm wide) and an outer band (8 cm wide). On this outer band seven anthropomorphic figures dressed as warriors are represented. Some of them have attributes that link them to warlike, star deities such as: Tlahuizcalpantecuhtli, identified by the drop-like designs on the headdresses, Huitzilopochtli, identified by the diadem with straight bars bifurcating at the top; and Mixcoatl, identified by the net basket. It is also likely that the headdress with circular and fusiform elements associates one of the figures with the maize god.

The position of the mosaic disc at the bottom of Offering 99 links it with the night-time journey of the stars through the earth's interior during the re-creation of the Mesoamerican underworld – one of the important functions of this journey was the underworld's fertilization.

The presence of some 226 projectile points in the offering, along with the remains of a roseate spoonbill (*Ajaia ajaja*) – called *quecholli* in Náhuatl – just above the disc, suggests the possibility that the offering was related to the Quecholli festival in the ritual calendar dedicated to Mixcoatl. This festival, in which a great number of arrows were made and offered to *Huitzilopochtli* and to warriors who had died in battle, commemorates the descent of the stars into the interior of the earth.

Adrián Velázquez and
Maria Eugenia Marín

94 Turquoise mosaic disc from the Templo Mayor, Tenochtitlán.

Another mosaic shield (fig. 95), also from a cave deposit in the Puebla region, was found in the late 1950s or early 1960s and is now in the Musées Royaux d'Art et d'Histoire, Brussels. The concentric bands of mosaic on this shield are very sharply defined; the level of each alternate band was raised very precisely by about a millimetre. Close examination shows that these differences of level were formed by careful carving of the underlying wood.[40] The tesserae were then fixed in place with a relatively thick (*c.*1–1.5 mm) layer of dark-coloured resin.

Some mosaic shields, for example those in the British Museum (fig. 92), Naturhistorisches Museum, Vienna (fig. 93), and the National Museum of the American Indian (Smithsonian Institution), Washington (fig. 96), display particularly complex designs. Despite the fact that all have lost their mosaic decoration to a greater or lesser extent, it is still possible to discern many of their original iconographic elements. The Washington shield is especially well preserved and the scene depicted appears to match that illustrated in the Codex Vaticanus,[41] where the descending figure can be identified as the goddess Xochiquetzal (the flower feather goddess and goddess of love) falling to earth (with the Toltecs underneath 'receiving sacrificial banners').[42]

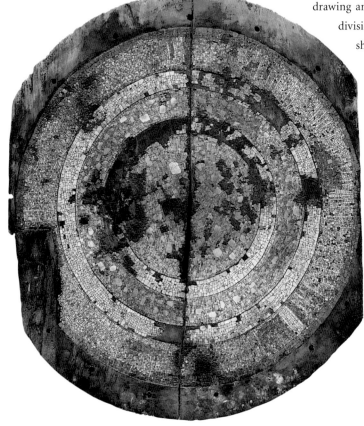

The mosaic design on the shield now in the British Museum (see drawing and overlay in figs 97, 98) portrays the principal divisions of the Aztec universe.[43] The overall circular shape of the shield corresponds to the surface of the earth. At its centre is a circle of mosaic, with four rays (fig. 98) still partially outlined by red *Spondylus princeps* and conch shell (fig. 99a); this is a solar disc. The four rays emanating from the solar disc divide the earth into four quarters. In each quarter stands a sky-bearer (fig. 99b), with eyes (fig. 99c), teeth and ear ornaments (fig. 99d) formed of mother-of-pearl shell. The hands are represented by incised mother-of-pearl and pitted orange *Spondylus* shell (fig. 99e).

Solar discs feature in the design of many shields and may reflect the association between Tonatiuh, the sun, and turquoise.

95 Turquoise mosaic shield from Puebla (diam. 45.5 cm).

Tonatiuh, among the most prominent of the sky gods, was central to the cult of war, which sought to obtain captives and hearts for sacrifice to the sun. The sun was often depicted as a warrior with a rayed solar disc, and the significance of solar discs on mosaic shields probably relates to the symbolism of warfare in their ceremonial use.

The shield also incorporates the image of a great serpent emerging from toothed jaws and coiling skywards. The tail of the serpent is plumed on its lowermost coil and the

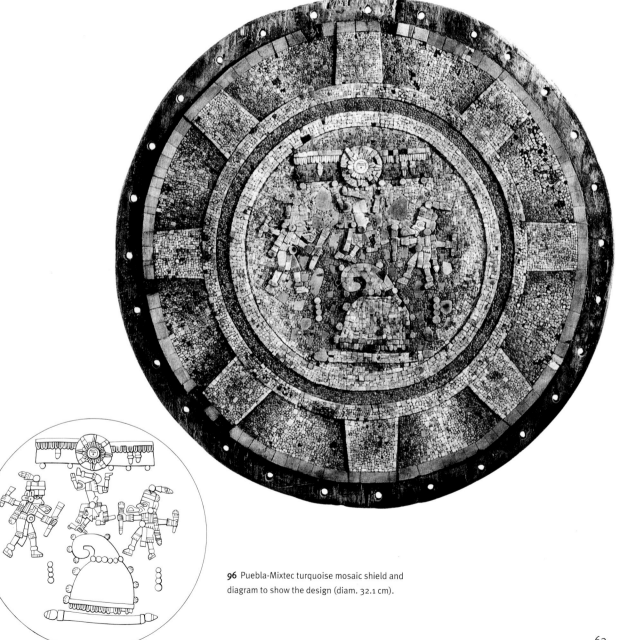

96 Puebla-Mixtec turquoise mosaic shield and diagram to show the design (diam. 32.1 cm).

head bears a large fang of white conch shell (fig. 99f). The eye is made from mother-of-pearl shell and the jaw is outlined using reddish-pink *Spondylus princeps* and conch shell. One side of the serpent's body is bordered by small studs of pine resin, the same resin that was used to fix the tesserae to the wood. Each of the studs was formed individually on top of the resin layer beneath and then covered by gold foil.[44] Some of the studs retain their original foils (fig. 99g), complete with the small folds and puckers in the gold that were inevitably formed when the flat foils were pressed over the domed studs.

The body of the serpent winds sinuously upward through the design (fig. 97). At the top are the flowering branches of a tree, the

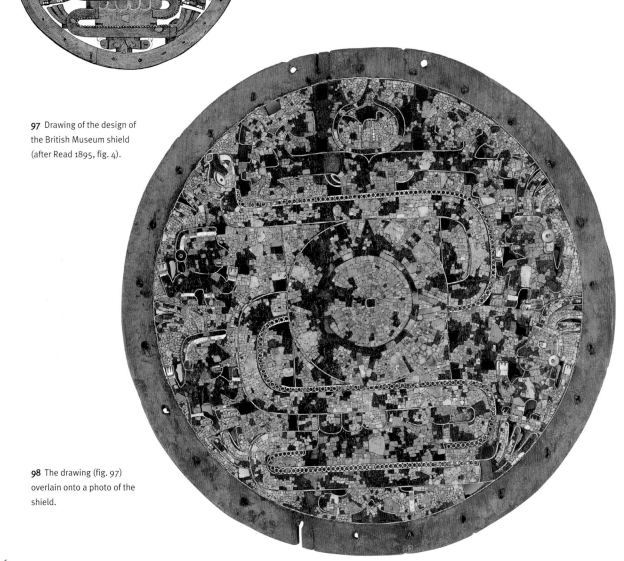

97 Drawing of the design of the British Museum shield (after Read 1895, fig. 4).

98 The drawing (fig. 97) overlain onto a photo of the shield.

64

(a)

(c)

(d)

(b) (e)

(f)

(g) (h)

99 Details from the British Museum shield: **(a)** slabs of red *Spondylus princeps* and *Strombus* shell; **(b)** one of the four sky-bearers; **(c)** the eye of a sky-bearer made of *Pinctada* mother-of-pearl shell; **(d)** ear ornament of *Pinctada* mother-of-pearl shell; **(e)** hands of sky-bearer, made from *Pinctada* mother-of-pearl and pitted orange *Spondylus* shell; **(f)** fang of the serpent, made from white *Strombus* shell; **(g)** original gold foil on the resin studs; **(h)** anthropomorphic mask.

trunk of which, hidden by a raised square 'cartouche', forms a vertical 'world axis' connecting the underworld and the earthly and celestial realms.[45] The ability of snakes to move freely between water, earth and the forest canopy probably accounts for their symbolic role in Mesoamerican mythology as an intermediary between the different layers of the cosmos. At the top of the tree there is an upturned anthropomorphic mask with raised hands (fig. 99h) implying that the tree can be seen as a metaphor for the king, who derives his authority on earth from divine sources of power and who would himself have carried the shield.

A feature of the shield's design is the use of surface relief to define the various iconographical features. Careful carving of the underlying wood, in this instance *Pinus* sp. (pine), established not just the overall shape but also the finer, three-dimensional features of the designs such as the serpent and the sky-bearers, which were raised by about a millimetre to outline their shapes better. The technique is a characteristic of several of the turquoise mosaics and appears to have been similar to that used to define the circular bands of the Brussels shield (fig. 95).

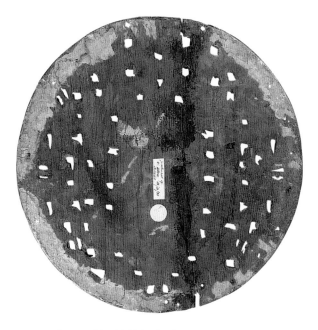

100 Reverse of the shield showing the numerous holes that penetrate it.

A band of now undecorated wood around the circumference of the shield is pierced by a series of more of less regularly spaced holes (see fig. 92), which might have been used to attach feathers to the shield. In addition, there are numerous holes in the body of the shield which, from the back appear to be located at random (fig. 100) but are in fact positioned and shaped very precisely to coincide with particular elements in the mosaic design (fig. 101). These must have been made before the mosaic work commenced, indicating that the final design was planned in detail prior to the tesserae being laid down.

Mosaic on a human skull

This mosaic (fig. 102) is usually identified with Tezcatlipoca, or Smoking Mirror, who, as one of four powerful creator deities, was among the most important gods in the Aztec pantheon. The name 'Smoking Mirror' derives from the Náhuatl word *tezapoctli*, meaning 'shining smoke'. Tezcatlipoca is conventionally cast as an adversary to Quetzalcoatl, the two gods being seen as opposing forces of darkness and light, evil and good. In illustrations in the codices (fig. 103) Tezcatlipoca is often depicted with obsidian mirrors at the head and in place of a torn-off foot.[46] He can also be identified by the three black bands: one at the forehead, another at the nose and the third at the chin.[47]

Other examples of mosaics overlaid on human skulls are known to have survived. In Aztec mythology there was a strong association between death and rebirth, and skulls with 'bright shining eyes' are thought to represent

101 Section of the shield with holes 'highlighted' in red, showing how they were carefully placed and shaped to coincide with particular elements in the design.

'the continuity of life after death'.[48] The skulls of sacrificial victims were placed on skull racks, or *tzompantli*, an example of which has been discovered opposite the Templo Mayor.

A Mixtec figure wearing a skull as part of his costume is illustrated in Codex Zouche-Nuttall (fig. 104) and in the Codex Telleriano-Remensis Aztec gods are depicted with such skulls tied around their waists at the back.[49] The long straps of deerskin leather attached to the mosaic of Tezcatlipoca (fig. 102) suggest that it, too, would have been worn in this way, probably by a deity impersonator.[50] Close examination shows that the straps were painted red, using an iron-rich ochre. Osteological

102 Turquoise mosaic of Tezcatlipoca on a human skull.

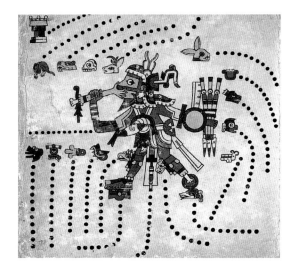

103 Tezcatlipoca, as shown on the final opening of the Codex Fejérváry-Mayer.

104 Deity from the Codex Zouche-Nuttall (p. 39) with a skull as part of his costume.

examination of the skull has been undertaken by Theya Molleson and Helen Liversidge and an extract from their report is given below.

> There is a very clean and smooth cut across the frontal bone of the skull. There is no apparent damage to the eye sockets (orbits) by the placement of the shell and pyrites, although the nasal area was damaged by the insertion of the shell plates for the nose. The lower jaw (mandible) is complete and appears to belong to the same individual as the face. Evidence from the teeth indicates a young to mature adult of about thirty years. Certain teeth are missing from the upper and lower jaws, some due to loss during life and others post-mortem. There is evidence that at least one tooth is misplaced: the lower central incisor, which is so spatulate, is an upper central incisor that has been 'implanted'. There is no evidence for any extensive damage to the face, such as a blow to the upper jaw. Features observed on the lower jaw and chin area as well as the sloping frontal and shape of the eye sockets suggest a male.
>
> Theya Molleson and Helen Liversidge

The back of the cranium was cut away before the mosaic was laid down, and some sawn surfaces of bone can be seen. Most of the rear of the skull is covered by a deerskin leather fitment (fig. 105), into which one end of each of the straps is bound. Some of the leather pieces are associated with thin cord made from maguey (agave) fibre. The lower jaw is hinged on the leather lining and remains movable. The features of the skull can be seen very clearly in the radiograph (fig. 106).

The striking, horizontal black bands across the face, characteristic of Tezcatlipoca, were created from tesserae of lignite, which contrast dramatically with the alternate bands of

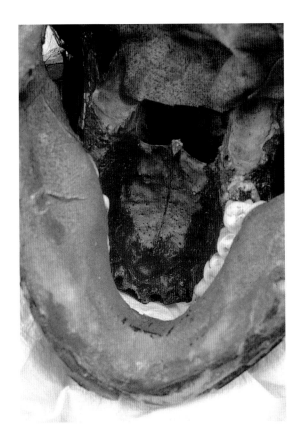

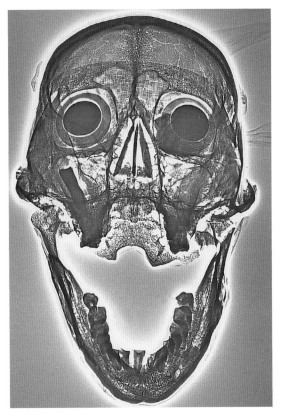

105 Part of the protective leather fitment on the back of the skull.

106 Xeroradiograph of the mosaic skull.

107 Tesserae of lignite.

108 The stark contrast of bright blue turquoise with dense black lignite; note how carefully the tesserae are shaped, so that they fit closely together.

109 A gap in the tessera revealing the underlying adhesive, in which the coarse grinding marks from the back of the missing tessera are imprinted.

110 Turquoise tesserae.

turquoise tesserae. Most of the lignite tesserae (fig. 107) are much larger (up to about 8 mm across) than the turquoise and, indeed, larger than tesserae used on other mosaics.

Nevertheless, the same high quality of workmanship is evident; the precision with which individual tesserae were cut to shape and placed can be seen very clearly in fig. 109.

The tesserae were stuck to the surface of the skull using dark brown pine resin adhesive. In some areas tesserae have been lost (see fig. 109). Here the adhesive beneath can be seen clearly and the edges of a lost bevelled tessera are imprinted on the surface. The adhesive has also taken a mould of the reverse of the lost tessera, revealing coarse grinding marks, possibly deliberate keying to improve adhesion.

The smaller turquoise tesserae are very uniform in colour (fig. 110), a stronger shade of blue than that found on other mosaics, where a much wider selection of turquoise colours was often used to highlight elements within the design or to create more subtle graduations. Clearly, the aim was to produce two simple bold blue bands to contrast with the black lignite.

The nasal cavity is dramatically highlighted by vivid coral-coloured, naturally pitted *Spondylus* shell, which lines the cavity and was used to reconstruct the nasal septum (fig. 111). The effect may have been intended to resemble a flayed head with the soft tissues removed. The contrast with the black lignite and bright blue turquoise tesserae is striking (see fig. 102); the suggestion of flaying provides further allusion to the association between death and rebirth.

The upper band of turquoise forms a vibrant blue background for the eyes. These ground and polished orbs of pyrite (fig. 112) are set in bright, white circles of carved and polished conch shell (fig. 113). In Aztec iconography eyes were closely associated with mirrors, which in Mesoamerica were often made from tessellated pyrite;[51] the pyrite orbs have taken on a rather dark, almost iridescent appearance, evoking the Smoking Mirror of Tezcatlipoca.

111 Detail of the nasal cavity where bright red *Spondylus* shell is used to dramatic effect.

112 A polished orb of pyrite forming one of the eyes.

113 Part of one of the white circles of carved and polished *Strombus* conch shell surrounding the pyrite eyes.

The knife

Knives are indelibly associated with ritual sacrifice in ancient Mesoamerica (fig. 114). Only a few knives with intact mosaic handles survive and these illustrate vividly how they became transformed into objects imbued with symbolic meaning.

Flint knives figure prominently in all Mesoamerican cultures. Flint is a very tough, hard material; it is shaped by chipping and flaking, a time-consuming and laborious process known as knapping. Very fine knives and blades were also made from obsidian (volcanic glass) – an ideal raw material for skilled workmanship, producing a razor-sharp edge. Flint blades of many different hues have been discovered during the excavations carried out recently at the Templo Mayor in Mexico City. Qualities such as colour and translucence may have played a part in determining the choice and range of raw material, but the knapping properties of the material were clearly paramount. Unhafted and undecorated flint blades, typically about 25 cm long, were frequently deposited in offering caches at the Templo Mayor.[52] In one instance they were uncovered essentially undisturbed as left by the Aztec priests arranged around the rim of a stone box as part of an offering to the rain god, Tlaloc.[53]

The Templo Mayor excavations have yielded other knives that are decorated on both sides with white flint and obsidian inlay depicting the eyes and teeth of a face in profile. In some cases these blades are set vertically in a lump of resin, in order to represent the glyph *tecpatl* ('flint', i.e. sacrificial knife) which is associated with one of the 'year-bearers' in the 260-day Aztec ritual calendar and the cardinal points – north, the direction of death and cold.

The finest examples of decorated knives are those that are hafted with elaborate mosaic handles. There are few surviving examples; more often than not the wooden handles have disintegrated or become separated from their blades and consequently any vestiges of applied decoration have been lost. The wooden handle of a rather similar

114 A scene from the Codex
Magliabechiano (lam. 66).

knife (see fig. 53) was found in Mexico City in the first half of the twentieth century; the
blade, though pre-Hispanic, was added as a reconstruction.[54] This knife lacks any trace
of applied decoration, but it is unclear whether this represents a haft to which mosaic
decoration would have been added or whether the carving in this instance completes the
decorative effect. It seems certain that, without their mosaic, hafts such as those in figs
29 and 118 would appear very similar.

The hafted knives, with their detailed carving and intricate mosaic designs, were part
of a world where inanimate instruments and tools become active 'ensouled' agents
wielding powers of life and death. There is ample evidence in the codices (fig. 114) and
from eyewitness Spanish accounts pointing to the role that these instruments played in
Aztec sacrificial rituals. Tough, sharp-edged flint blades would have been used to pierce
the chests of sacrificial captives and to extract their hearts for presentation to the gods.
Cortés described some aspects of the ritual, which involved taking blood from the hearts
removed from living sacrificial victims and mixing it with flour made by grinding up all
the local types of seeds and vegetables. The blood and flour mixture was then used to
make large idols; once these were completed, the priests offered up more hearts and
smeared blood on the faces of the idols.[55]

The xeroradiograph of the knife (fig. 29) reveals the part of the flint blade that
lies within the haft, just under 25 per cent of its total length. The blade appears to have
been sharply tapered for insertion into the haft. It is a fine example of the sophisticated

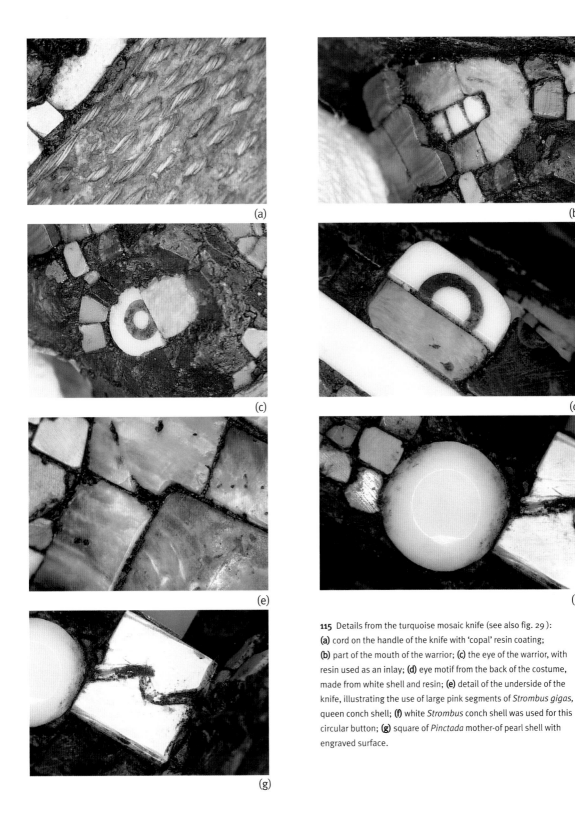

115 Details from the turquoise mosaic knife (see also fig. 29):
(a) cord on the handle of the knife with 'copal' resin coating;
(b) part of the mouth of the warrior; **(c)** the eye of the warrior, with resin used as an inlay; **(d)** eye motif from the back of the costume, made from white shell and resin; **(e)** detail of the underside of the knife, illustrating the use of large pink segments of *Strombus gigas*, queen conch shell; **(f)** white *Strombus* conch shell was used for this circular button; **(g)** square of *Pinctada* mother-of pearl shell with engraved surface.

116 The face of the warrior can be seen emerging from the beak of the eagle costume.

technique of pressure-flaking, which was used to remove shallow flakes over the surface of the honey-coloured blade. The haft was bound tightly with maguey (agave) fibre cord (fig. 115a), coated with a pale yellow, translucent 'copal' resin from *Protium* sp. However, this binding is laid over the wood rather than the blade, so it is unclear how much of a part it would have played in holding the blade firmly in place. Indeed, when viewed on the radiograph the blade appears to be rather insecurely positioned in the haft, raising the question of how effectively it would perform as a knife; possibly its cere-monial role was entirely symbolic. No traces of blood were found on either the blade or the cord.

The handle of the knife was carved from a single piece of *Cedrela odorata* wood, fash-ioned into the form of a crouching man wearing the regalia of an eagle warrior. He clasps the haft of the knife with both hands in front of him; his face is framed by the beak of the eagle headdress, the wings of which cover his shoulders (fig. 116). In Aztec mythology the eagle represented the power of the day and was believed to carry the sun into the sky from the underworld each morning. Eagle costumes were worn by the prestigious fighters 'of the daytime': the eagle warriors; fig. 117 shows an eagle warrior illustrated in the Codex Zouche-Nuttall.

Two very similar wooden knife handles with mosaic are in the collections of the Museo Nazionale Preistorico-Etnografico 'L. Pigorini' in Rome. One of these takes the

117 Eagle warrior. Codex Zouche-Nuttall, p. 11.

form of a figure in much the same crouching position, again grasping the handle of the knife (fig. 118). The costume is rather different, however, and includes a headdress, ear ornaments, sandals, bracelets and a skirt. It has not been linked with any particular deity or elite individual.[56] The other knife handle in these collections is rather similar in concept and has an animal head with open mouth.[57] All of these decorated knives display the exceptional craftsmanship of the Aztec-Mixtec artisans.

On the eagle warrior knife the tesserae of turquoise, malachite and shell were applied to the wood using an adhesive made from a mixture of two plant resins in roughly equal proportions. One component was pine resin, which has been identified on most of the other mosaics. The other, *Protium* resin, is the same 'copal' resin that was used to coat the cord that binds the haft of the knife.

The careful attention to detail – a characteristic of all the turquoise mosaics – can be appreciated from an examination of the face of the warrior framed by the open beak of the eagle costume (fig. 116). Across the forehead there are bands of white shell and dark green malachite, parts of which are now missing. The teeth, also of white shell, and each only a

118 Handle of a sacrificial knife (h 5 x w 12.5 cm).

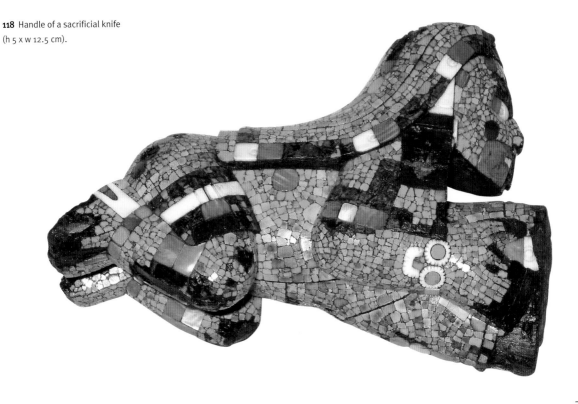

119 The back of the warrior's eagle costume, showing the dramatic use of white shell with malachite.

millimetre wide, contrast sharply with the surrounding lips (or gums) formed from tesserae of orange-red shell (fig. 115b). Both the white and orange-coloured shell used here can be found in different species of conch. The dark green nose plug, made from distinctly banded malachite, covers part of the mouth and is very similar to the one worn by the figure on the knife handle shown in fig. 118. The eyes of the warrior, formed from white conch shell, are scarcely more than 2 mm across, yet on each a circular groove has been carefully engraved and inlaid with resin (fig. 115c). The orange of the eyes is formed from the same orange conch shell that was used for the mouth. The eyes on the knife in fig. 118 were created with a very similar technique, but without inlay.

Much of the mosaic on the lower arms of the eagle warrior is missing, and although on the left wrist there is a wide band of pink shell with malachite, no tesserae resembling the elaborate bracelet worn by the figure forming the handle of the knife in the Rome collection survive. The hands, which grasp the end of the blade, have lost much of their mosaic decoration but sufficient remains to show the careful use of pink and orange conch shell and dark green malachite to mark out nails at the end of each finger. The mosaic that covers the hafting of the blade behind the cord is worked in fine tesserae of pale blue-green turquoise, carefully applied so that it presents a smooth surface that curves around the haft.

Turquoise is used rather sparingly over much of the remainder of the warrior, in particular on the eagle costume. On the back of the costume geometric white conch shell segments are vividly combined with dark green malachite (fig. 119). The eye motif is repeated here and elsewhere in the form of white and orange shell; the semi-circular grooves in the white shell are inlaid with resin (fig. 115d). The similarity of these 'eyes' with those that appear in the codices is striking. On the wings and beak of the headdress there are large pink segments from queen conch shells. The underside of this knife (fig. 120) is rarely displayed or illustrated; here the pink conch shell is used in a bold rectangular block to cover much of the 'belly' area (fig. 115e) and is outlined by small yellow

120 Underside of the knife.

orange tesserae from *Spondylus* shells. Although substantial areas of mosaic on the upper part of the legs are missing, evidence of alternating white shell and malachite does survive in places, and matching bands across the lower part of the belly suggest that the costume included a stripy garment in similar colours to that worn on the back.

A few small, circular, 'button-shaped', white conch shell pieces (fig. 115f) remain around one of the ankles; imprints in resin indicate that there was originally a complete band of these on both legs. Circular pieces of mother-of-pearl shell are applied in much the same way on the knife in fig. 119; a different kind of mother-of-pearl shell (*Pinctada mazatlantica*) provides a square-cut and incised tessera (fig. 115g) above the left foot of the eagle warrior.

Eagle warriors along with jaguar warriors formed the two main military orders, schooled in the arts of war in special precincts within the heart of Tenochtitlán. Young men earned recognition and enhanced their status by performing feats of bravery and daring. By securing captives for sacrifice, warriors could achieve different levels of recognition, depending on the numbers captured. Status was marked by the award of special insignia, including helmets, shields and elaborately decorated cloaks, like the eagle cloak worn by the warrior depicted on the knife handle.[58] Mosaic knives may also have formed an essential part of this ritual regalia.

121 Turquoise mosaic figure of a jaguar.

The jaguar

Although the identity of this seated animal with open mouth and protruding tongue (fig. 121) is not certain it has always been interpreted as representing a jaguar. At least two other jaguar mosaics are known – both were in the Museum für Völkerkunde, Berlin.[59] Both of the Berlin jaguars had open mouths with fangs; possibly the jaguar in fig. 121 also had teeth originally.

Hunting by night, the jaguar was seen as representing danger and darkness, and as a religious icon it was both feared and revered. Along with the eagle, the jaguar symbolized power and courage and was associated with the elite warriors of Aztec society. Both were linked with the course of the sun: the eagle, a daytime hunter, represented the sun as it passed across the sky, while the jaguar was thought to supply blood to the sun as it travelled through the underworld during the night.[60]

The main function of the elite eagle and jaguar warriors was to deliver victims who could be sacrificed to provide nourishment, in the form of blood, to the sun. Representations of jaguars and eagles, and other images that evoked death, were applied to *cuauhxicalli*, stone vessels that were used to receive offerings of hearts and blood.[61]

122 Details from the jaguar: **(a)** an oval design within the mosaic; **(b)** dark green malachite surrounding polished pyrite in another design; **(c)** engraved *Pinctada* mother-of-pearl shell, perhaps used here to simulate 'silver' fur.

A colossal stone sculpture of a jaguar, found close to the Templo Mayor in Mexico City,[62] has on its back a cylindrical cavity believed to have contained sacrificial offerings.

The mosaic jaguar in fig. 121 was decorated with tesserae fixed in place with pine resin. It appears that the surface has been treated at some time with a drying oil, and in the course of this treatment, the pine resin has partially dissolved, destroying the impressions of lost tesserae that are preserved on other mosaics. Nevertheless, several circular and oval designs can still be discerned within the mosaic (fig. 122a) – their shapes accentuated by the use of tesserae of darker blue turquoise. Despite its poor condition, the carving of the jaguar is particularly expressive and animated, though this may have been obscured when the mosaic was intact.

The surviving tesserae suggest that the mosaic design was complex. On the haunches of the animal elongate oval designs formed from dark green malachite surround polished tesserae of pyrite (fig. 122b). The circular rosettes may reflect the natural spotted patterning that is seen in the jaguar's pelt, and it has been suggested that the oval features that include shiny 'metallic' pyrite may represent mirrors.[63] Similar rosettes featured on the double-headed jaguar that was in Berlin.[64]

Mother-of-pearl shell was applied to the underbelly (figs 122c, 123) and elsewhere on the figure in relatively large engraved pieces. The technique is very similar to the way in which mother-of-pearl was used to represent the sheen of fur on a Post-Classic Toltec mosaic head of a coyote warrior from Tula (fig. 124). The eye sockets are now empty but may have contained pyrite orbs like the jaguar skull excavated at Kaminaljuyu that has pyrite set into the eye sockets.[65]

The jaguar was made from *Cedrela odorata* wood like most of the turquoise mosaic objects now in the British Museum. The xeroradiograph in fig. 125 shows a break

123 Side view of the jaguar showing mother-of-pearl 'fur'.

124 Head of a coyote warrior.

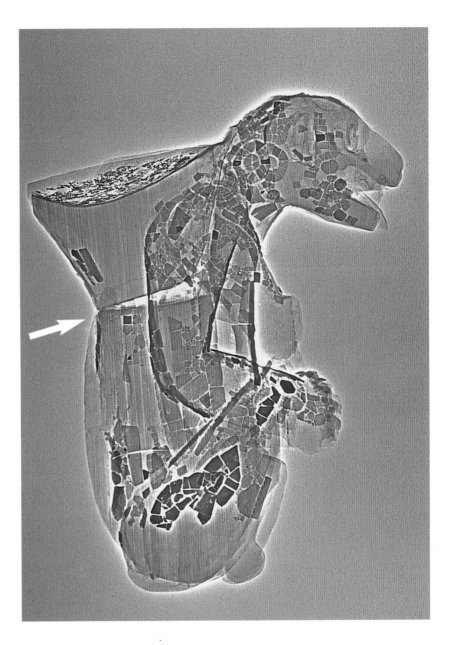

125 Xeroradiograph of the jaguar showing a join in the wood used to form the base.

across the longitudinal grain of the wood. In the radiograph the textured appearance of the container bowl carried on the back of the jaguar indicates the presence of small flakes of dense metal; chemical analysis using XRF confirmed that these are gold. It seems that the bowl was either fully gilded or perhaps embellished with fine flakes of gold scattered across the concave surface. The function of the bowl is unclear: it may have been intended to receive offerings and it seems too shallow to have functioned as any kind of vessel.

126 Turquoise mosaic animal head.

127 Details of the animal head: **(a)** distinctive yellow-striped, white *Strombus* conch shell forming the surrounds to the pyrite eyes; **(b)** the seed pearls of the 'eyebrows'; **(c)** the suspension loop of conch shell; **(d)** one of the sharp shark's teeth lining the jaws; **(e)** plates of garnet, set in beeswax, lining the roof of the mouth; **(f)** some of the beads in the lower jaw, one of which has a drill-hole running through its centre.

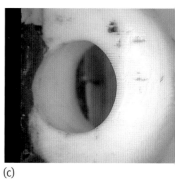

(a) (b) (c)

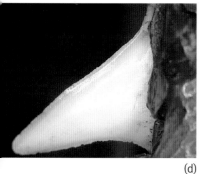

(d) (e) (f)

The animal head

Although this mosaic (fig. 126) has been generally referred to as an 'animal head', the type of animal represented has long been problematic. It has been variously described as 'an ape-like head'[66] and a 'monkey-head',[67] and 'from some angles it strongly suggests a fish head'.[68] A rather similar head, now in the Museum für Völkerkunde, Vienna,[69] has been described as a 'Mirror frame ... head of a predator, feline or canine'.

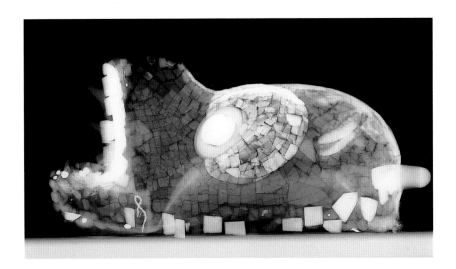

128 The radiograph of the animal head: note the wire (bright white) at the back of the lower jaw and the faint shadows beneath the pearl eyebrows that may indicate the remains of earlier 'ears'.

The animal head (fig. 126) was formed on a wooden base and the tesserae set in place with pine resin. The soft, rather pale yellow to white wood is similar to the coral tree (*Erythrina americana* or *E. coralloides*, known locally as *colorín*). Microscopical examination revealed a spongy cellular structure but did not yield any diagnostic features to confirm the identification as *colorín* wood. The smoothly curved surface that forms the 'face' was set with pale blue tesserae of turquoise. Dark green malachite tesserae delimit the surrounds for the eyes, which are formed by polished orbs of pyrite and surrounded by annular pieces of yellow-striped, white conch shell (fig. 127a). Above each of the eyes, forming 'eyebrows', are arcs of small seed pearls (fig. 127b). The use of these appears to be unique to this mosaic. Furthermore, they are set in beeswax, which was not the usual choice of adhesive on the mosaics that we have examined. The radiograph of this object suggests that the seed pearls may not have formed part of the original design. There are indications that the head once had ears, but at some time these have been damaged; on the radiograph the broken fragments can be seen within the wood underneath the 'eyebrows' (fig. 128).

The radiograph also reveals the presence of what appears to be a twisted metal wire concealed within the lower jaw; and it is possible that it may once have had a tongue, perhaps of orange *Spondylus* shell like that of the Vienna head and similarly operated by a wire inserted into the mouth through the lower jaw.

A ring of white conch shell was set into the top of the head. This could have been used as a suspension loop enabling the object to be worn as a pendant (fig. 127c). The Vienna animal head was similarly fitted with a loop of leather. The backs of both animal heads are hollow and it is thought that each would have been set with a mirror.

In addition to the seed pearls, some unusual materials were used in the mouth of the animal head (fig. 129). The jaws are lined with small sharply pointed shark's teeth (fig. 127d), and although sharks are not uncommon in the seas to the east or west of Mexico, this is the only recorded use of shark's teeth on mosaic objects. The roof of the mouth is set with flat, polished plates of red garnet (fig. 127e), and in the lower jaw there are many small polished stones, some rounded and others faceted. These have been identified as emerald, beryl, spinel and zircon.[70] Many appear to have been roughly polished beads; one has a drill-hole (fig. 127f). Although various precious stones are mentioned in the inventories of treasure sent to Spain, they do not seem to

129 The mouth of the animal head.

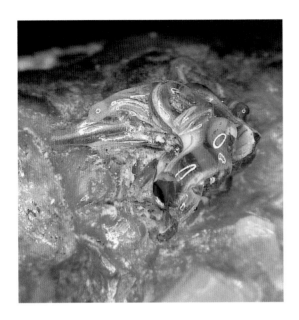

130 A fragment of yellow-green glass, which must be a post-Conquest addition.

have been used on other mosaics. Among the gemstones are small fragments with the appearance of gold, but which XRF analysis has shown to be brass, an alloy that was not known to the Aztecs.

All of these unusual materials, like the seed pearls, are set with beeswax, and the workmanship is of inferior quality to the rest of the piece. These observations indicate post-Conquest modification or reconstruction of this object.[71] Further evidence, in the form of fragments of yellow-green glass (fig. 130), suggests that the changes were made after the arrival of the object in Europe. Glass was not made in Mexico before the Conquest, so that there can be no doubt that these fragments must have been attached to the mosaic afterwards. It is reported that Grijalva 'gave to the Indians some glass beads, some green and others yellow' [72] in exchange for the rich gifts sent by Motecuhzoma, and it is tempting to suggest that the green and yellow glass on the mosaic may have come from this source. However, analysis of a minute fragment of the glass in the SEM has suggested that while the glass may be of fifteenth- to seventeenth-century date, it is probably of Italian, rather than Spanish origin.[73] This may indicate that the glass was not among the glass beads carried from Spain by Grijalva but was added to the object in an Italian workshop.[74]

Epilogue

In 1994 the nine turquoise mosaics went on permanent display in the British Museum's new Mexico gallery. Instantly recognizable and alluring, they are iconic objects that have inspired the reproduction of images and designs for merchandise ranging from T-shirts to ties. In 2003 the 'warty' mask featured on a postage stamp issued to mark the 250th anniversary of the British Museum, reflecting the status of the mosaics within the Museum's collections. Their enduring appeal is due, no doubt, to a fascination with precious materials and admiration for the astonishing quality of craftsmanship, but perhaps above all to their compelling significance in the Aztec world.

Notes

CHAPTER 1

1 The nine turquoise mosaics in the British Museum collections have previously been discussed by Pasztory (1983) and Carmichael (1970), who in her introduction expressed the hope that a subsequent publication would discuss the materials and technology of the mosaics.

2 The term 'Aztec' is principally used to refer to the indigenous peoples settled around Lake Texcoc in the Valley of Mexico who referred to themselves as the Mexica.

3 Boone (2000), pp. 10–11.

4 Boone (2000), p. 251.

5 Suggested areas of origin for the Borgia codices are Puebla-Tlaxcala near the Valley of Mexico and the south-central Mixtec region (Byland 1993, p. xiv).

6 Berdan and Anawalt (1992).

7 Sahagún (1950–82).

8 Durán (1994).

9 Martyr (1912).

10 Martyr (1912), vol. II, p. 20.

11 Oviedo (1851–5), as translated by Saville (1922), p. 7.

12 López de Gómara (1964), cited by Carmichael (1970), p. 17.

13 Seler (1904), p. 412.

14 As noted by Carmichael (1970), p. 25.

15 Cortés was preoccupied with securing as much gold as possible, which the Spaniards valued more for the intrinsic worth of the metal itself rather than for the beauty and workmanship invested in the objects. Thus, many fine cast gold artefacts were destroyed and melted down into gold bars or ingots, which were more convenient to transport. One such ingot was discovered in 1982, during excavations underneath buildings belonging to the Bank of Mexico in Mexico City.

16 Martyr (1912), vol. II, p. 197.

17 Saville (1922), pp. 20, 21.

18 Dürer (1995), p. 47.

19 Pasztory (1990/91), pp. 105–6. See also Feest (1990).

20 Coe (1994), pp. 187–8.

21 Pogue (1915). The mosaics from Berlin, referred to by Pogue and illustrated by Saville (1922, pl. XVIII skull, pl. XXXII a jaguar head, and pl. XXXIV a two-headed jaguar figure) and by Seler (1904, vol IV, p. 366, figs cat 4014, 7159 and 7160), were destroyed during World War II. However, the Ethnologisches Museum in Berlin holds in its collections several other turquoise mosaic artefacts that were shown at the *Azteken* exhibition in Berlin (2003) and illustrated in the catalogue (Matos Moctezuma and Solís Olguín 2003, see cats 24–7). We are grateful to Marie Gaida for this information.

22 However, it is possible that they were later discoveries from dry caves in southern Puebla or northern Oaxaca during the colonial period. Recent examples of such material include the Cueva Cheve wooden tablet discovered in the Cuiatec region of Oaxaca in 1989 (Steele and Snavely 1997), which depicts a battle scene in detailed turquoise mosaic. Looting of tombs and caves in this region was rife throughout the colonial period as noted by Caso (1965, p. 915).

23 Warwick Bray, pers. comm. This mask, made of turquoise and red *Spondylus* shell on a wooden base, was illustrated by Berjonneau *et al.* (1985), ill. 181; see also Dallas Museum of Art (1997), p. 193.

24 Kavanagh (1987).

25 Christy's interest in the antiquities of Mexico was triggered by his travels there. In 1859 he purchased the three turquoise mosaics from the collection of Mr Bram Hertz at a sale at Sotheby and Wilkinson; they were the skull mosaic (purchased for £40), the 'warty' mask (£32) and the knife (£41)(King 1997). Of these, the 'warty' mask and the knife were thought by Hertz to have come from a collection in Florence from which they had been sold around 1830–40 (Carmichael 1970, p. 37). An Italian provenance for the knife was also suggested by Read (1895, pp. 387–8), who considered that it had been in the collection of Ferdinando Cospi and had been figured in the *Museo Cospiano*

(Bologna, 1667), along with the rather similar knife (which lacks its blade) now in Rome (see chapter 3). The skull was said by Hertz to have come from a collection in Bruges; this was taken by Tylor (1861) to imply that it could have been there since the Conquest, but Feest (1990, p. 35 and n. 56) has commented that this claim is not supported by the documentary evidence.

26 Several of the turquoise mosaics that were subsequently added to the British Museum collection may also have had 'Italian connections'. William Adams, the dealer from whom the shield was purchased in 1866, indicated that it had come from Turin. Adams also supplied the animal head to Augustus Franks (Keeper of British and Medieval Antiquities and Ethnography in the British Museum), indicating that this had come from northern Italy – the animal head was presented to the Museum by Franks in 1868. The serpent mask, purchased in 1870, has been linked (although somewhat tentatively) with a Medici inventory of the mid-17th century (Carmichael 1970, p. 36, quoting Walter Lehmann). The provenance of the remaining three mosaics – the figure of the jaguar (presented to the Museum in 1877 by Franks, who had purchased it from the Liverpool collector, Joseph Mayer), the helmet (bought in Paris by Franks and presented to the Museum in 1893) and the serpent (purchased by the Museum in 1894) – is not known. For more details of the European history of the objects see Carmichael (1970), pp. 34–6.

27 Coe and Diehl (1980); Evans (2004), p. 107.

28 Weigand and Weigand (2001), pp. 185–7.

29 Drucker *et al.* (1959); Evans (2004), pp. 174–7.

30 Each pavement is buried some five metres below present ground level. The one under the south-west mound measures 5 x 6.5m. See Freidel *et al.* (1993), pp. 132–7, on the significance of the ceremonial precinct as a portal to the subterranean underworld and the example of the pavement of closely fitting stones in

the sunken ball court at the Maya site of Tonina (Martin and Grube 2000: 1982).

31 Martínez Donjuán (1994), p. 160.

32 Evans (2004), pp. 263–4.

33 Evans (2004), pp. 282–3.

34 Berjonneau et al. (1985), pl. 143.

35 Saburo Sugiyama, pers. comm.

36 Evans (2004), pp. 130–1.

37 See Arqueología Mexicana 16 (2004). Many of these were recently brought together in an exhibition at the Museo Nacional de Antropología.

38 See Martin and Grube (2000), p. 113.

39 Martin and Grube (2000), pp. 48–9.

40 Schmidt (2004), p. 32.

41 This building was excavated and restored by Jorge R. Acosta during the 1940s and 1950s; see Mastache and Cobean (2003) and Cobean and Mastache (forthcoming).

42 The mosaic was fixed originally to a wooden frame, which had almost totally disintegrated, necessitating careful study and restoration (see Magar Meurs et al., n.d.)

43 Cobean and Mastache (2003), p. 57.

44 Taube (n.d.). Mosaic mirrors of pyrite and also of hematite were shown in two recent exhibitions, Courtly Art of the Ancient Maya (Miller and Martin, 2004, pls 15 and 16) and The Origins of Sacred Maya Kingship (Fields and Reents-Budet, 2005, pls 7–9), and their significance discussed.

45 Magar Meurs et al. (n.d.); Matos Moctezuma (1988); Cobean and Mastache (forthcoming); Taube (n.d.).

46 These were illustrated by Maudslay (1895–1902); see pl. 46 for the warrior shown in fig. 12.

47 Harbottle and Weigand (1992); Weigand and Weigand (2001), p. 187.

48 Winter and Macías (2001); see also Montero, 1968.

49 Coggins and Shane (1984), p. 113; Barrera Vásquez (1980).

50 A bright green variety of feldspar.

51 Graulich (1997, pp. 48, 69, 261) has linked these materials to the tonali, or spark, that gives life to humans.

52 Evans (2004), p. 364.

53 Sahagún (1950–82), Bk 11, p. 234.

54 Evans (2004), pp. 13, 260.

55 Carrasco (1982), Florescano (1999) and Graulich (1997).

56 Weigand and Weigand (2001), pp. 188–9

57 Sahagún (1950–82), Bk 9, pp. 60, 59.

58 Pohl (1994), pp. 83–93.

59 Sahagún (1950–82), Bk 9, p. 84.

CHAPTER 2

1 For a full account and technical details of analysis of the resins from the mosaics see Stacey et al. (2006).

2 The relationships between foreign trade, tribute and marketplace exchange in Aztec society were complex and are beyond the scope of this book, but this topic has been discussed elsewhere: see, for example, Anawalt (1998); Berdan (1982, 2002); Townsend (1992); Weigand and Weigand (2001).

3 Pogue (1915), p. 96.

4 Blake (1858).

5 See publications by Harbottle and Weigand (1992); also Mathien (1981, 2001). A different analytical approach that involves measuring the ratios between the different isotopes of lead (present at low levels in turquoise) has given encouraging results but more work is needed to characterize the potential geological sources; see Young et al. (1994).

6 For a recent commentary see Weigand and Weigand (2001).

7 Sahagún (1950–82), Bk 11, p. 222.

8 Sahagún (1950–82), Bk 11, p. 224.

9 Pohl (2001), p. 93.

10 Pohl (2001), p. 96.

11 Sahagún (1950–82), Bk 11, p. 228.

12 Sahagún (1950–82), Bk 11, p. 233.

13 Sahagún (1950–82), Bk 11, p. 233.

14 Morán-Zenteno (1994), p. 69; Panczner (1987), pp. 209–16.

15 Berdan and Anawalt (1992), p. 86.

16 Berdan and Anawalt (1992).

17 Sahagún (1950–82), Bk 11, p. 234.

18 Saville (1922), pp. 7, 20.

19 Arnold and Bohor (1975).

20 See José-Yacamán et al. (1996) and Polette et al. (2002) for details.

21 For a discussion on the procurement and trade of Pacific Spondylus especially, see Paulsen (1974); Marcos (1978) and Pillsbury (1994).

22 Sahagún (1950–82), Bk 10, p. 27.

23 Motte-Frorac (1996), p. 225.

24 Sahagún (1950–82), Bk 11, p. 107.

25 Sahagún (1950–82), Bk 1, p. 37.

26 Motte-Frorac (1996).

27 Sahagún (1950–82), Bk 10, p. 88.

28 Mills and White (1994), pp. 103–4.

29 Hernández (1943), pp. 530–48.

30 Martinez-Cortes (1970), p. 40.

31 Standley (1923), pp. 543–52.

32 Dressler (1953), p. 145.

33 Sahagún (1950–82), Bk 10, p. 26.

34 Mason (1929), p. 172; Montero (1968), p. 102.

35 Sahagún (1950–82), Bk 10, p. 88.

36 Harbottle and Weigand (1992).

37 Saville (1922), p. 76.

38 Sahagún (1950–82), Bk 9, pp. 73–4.

39 Martyr (1912), p. 197.

40 We are grateful to Sue Scott for sending us a copy of her essay 'Mosaic Masks from Mexico' on file at the Smithsonian Cultural Resources Center, Washington DC. In this she describes masks from two caches along with a further set of about thirty masks.

41 Durán (1994), pp. 417–30.

42 Sahagún (1950–82), Bk 9, p. 82.

43 Sahagún (1950–82), Bk 9, p. 82.

44 Sahagún (1950–82), Bk 10, p. 26.

45 For example, Harbottle and Weigand (1992).

46 Cartwright (1988).

47 Howes (1949), p. 141.

48 Berdan and Anawalt (1992).

49 Martyr (1912), vol. II, p. 197.

CHAPTER 3

1 Important previous descriptions of these mosaics have been given by Read (1895), Saville (1922), Pasztory (1983) and Carmichael (1970).

2 Martyr (1912), p. 197.

3 Ixtlilxochitl (1891–2), vol. 1, p. 351. We are grateful to Warwick Bray for providing this information.

4 The body would have been cremated at the end of this ceremony so it is unlikely that the royal funerary mask would have survived. Where burial practice involved the placing of mummy bundles in dry caves, as in Tehuacan Valley, survival of the masks is much more likely (see, for example, Pohl 1994).

5 See article by Leonardo López Luján (2002), who refers to a passage in Sahagún (Book 9) that can be interpreted as describing how to locate and recover relics from earlier civilizations.

6 Museo Nacional de Antropología, Mexico: CONACULTA-INAH, 10–9630. Matos Moctezuma and Solis Olguín (2002), cat. 13 (Felipe Solis and Robertos Velasco Alonso).

7 Matos Moctezuma and Solis Olguín (2002), cats 49 (Christina Elson), 52 (Felipe Solis and Robertos Velasco Alonso), and 53 (Gillett G. Griffin).

8 Vargas (1989); see Matos Moctezuma and Solis Olguín (2002), p. 475.

9 See illustration in Moctezuma and Olguín (2002), cat. 302 (Felipe Solis and Robertos Velasco Alonso).

10 Miller and Taube (1993), pp. 189–90.

11 McEwan (1994), p. 70.

12 For example, see Berjonneau et al. (1985), pl. 182.

13 Carmichael (1970), p. 21. See also King (1997), n.12.

14 See, for example, Berjonneau et al. (1985), pl. 182.

15 Caso (1969), pp. 164–5.

16 Even a foil this thin is about ten times the thickness of gold leaf. The composition of the gold foil, approximately 75 parts gold/25 parts silver (with no copper), suggests that unrefined gold may have been used; for further discussion of Mexican goldwork, see, for example, La Niece and Meeks (2000).

17 These teeth are the third and the sixth from the left in fig. 59, and may be composed of one of the numerous synthetic materials, such as celluloid, that were developed in the late nineteenth century and used as substitutes for ivory.

18 Read (1895), p. 397.

19 For photographs of examples see Berjonneau et al. (1985), pl. 182; Fields and Zamudio-Taylor (2001), p. 188.

20 For an illustration of this piece see Fields and Zamudio-Taylor (2001), p. 188.

21 McEwan (1994), p. 70. See also Berjonneau et al. (1985). We are grateful to Warwick Bray for the Berjonneau reference.

22 Carmichael (1970), p. 25.

23 We are grateful to Berete Due and Espen Wehle for facilitating examination and imagery of this object.

24 Carmichael (1970), p. 33. Painted helmet masks are still in use in west and north-west Mexico as well as in Puebla Katsina ceremonialism (pers. comm. Phil Weigand).

25 Saville (1922) was more specific about these features, suggesting they represent the upper mandibles of eagles.

26 Richard Townsend, pers. comm. For an illustration of panaches see, for example, Pasztory (1983), col. pl. 12, showing an image of Nezahualpilli, Ruler of Texcoco, from the Codex Ixtlilxochitl.

27 Miller and Taube (1993), p. 148.

28 Miller and Taube (1993), pp. 149–50.

29 Pasztory (1983), pp. 233–4.

30 At least one of the teeth and possibly one of the fangs in the upper jaw of the left (true left) head is not made of shell; they appear to be glass-fibre replacements. A glass-fibre tooth is also present in the lower jaw of the right head accompanied by what appears to be a painted tessera of glass fibre in the gum area; the fangs on this side may also be glass-fibre replacements.

31 Illustrated in Poster and Fane (2000). We are grateful to Warwick Bray for this reference.

32 See ch. 1, n. 21.

33 Museum Reg. no. 43-382, Ambras collection. See Matos Moctezuma and Solis Olguín (2002), cat. 334 (Gerard van Bussel).

34 See for example Matos Moctezuma and Solis Olguín (2002), cat. 208 (Maria Gaida).

35 Townsend (1992), p. 191, quoting Sahagún (1950–82), Bk 1, pp. 1–2.

36 Anonymous Conqueror (1917), p. 22.

37 Saville (1922), p. 69.

38 See Feest (1990) for description and discussion of this and other Mexican items now in Vienna.

39 Saville (1922) and Sue Scott, pers. comm.

40 We are grateful for Sergio Purin for facilitating our examination of the shield.

41 Codex Vaticanus A, pl. 7.

42 Graulich (1997), p. 65.

43 Townsend (1979), pp. 38–9.

44 Non-destructive analysis of the gold, using X-ray fluorescence directly on the object, showed it to contain some silver and a little copper: Au 87%, Ag 12%, Cu 1%.

45 Townsend (1992), p. 118.

46 Carmichael (1970), p. 12.

47 In the codices Tezcatlipoca's black stripes are typically set against a yellow coloured face rather than the blue of the mosaic used here, and the identification of the skull with Tezcatlipoca has been questioned on this basis (Cecelia Klein, pers. comm.).

48 Locke (2002), p. 205.

49 Elizabeth Boone, pers. comm.

50 Elizabeth Bonne, pers. comm.

51 Taube (1992), pp. 169–204; Miller and Taube (1993), pp. 114–15.

52 López Luján (1994).

53 Matos Moctezuma and Solis Olguín (2002), cat. 265 (Eduardo Matos Moctezuma).

54 Matos Moctezuma and Solis Olguín (2002), cat. 153 (Felipe Solís and Roberto Velasco Alonso).

55 Cortés (1908), vol. 1, p. 262.

56 Matos Moctezuma and Solis Olguín (2002), cat. 295 (Carlo Nobile).

57 See Saville (1922), pl. xxxix.

58 See, for example, Pasztory (1983) for an account of eagle warriors, etc.

59 See ch. 1, n.21.

60 See, for example, Pasztory (1983), pp. 82, 233; Miller and Taube (1993), p. 102.

61 Solis Olguín (2002), p. 226.

62 See, for example, Pasztory (1983), p. 171.

63 Frances Berdan, pers. comm.

64 See ch. 1, n.21.

65 Miller and Taube (1993), p. 102.

66 Read (1895), p. 395.

67 Saville (1922), pl.XXXIII.

68 Carmichael (1970), p. 28.

69 Museum reg. no. 43-382, Ambras collection. Matos Moctezuma and Solis Olguín (2002), cat. 334 (Gerard van Bussel). See also Feest (1990). We are grateful to Gerard van Bussel for facilitating our examination of the animal head.

70 We are grateful to Sylvia Humphrey for these identifications.

71 Feest (1990), in his review of the evidence concerning the provenance of the animal head (and other objects) in Vienna, concluded that this was of colonial manufacture.

72 See Saville (1922), p. 12.

73 We are grateful to Colleen Stapleton for this analysis and interpretation.

74 There is little firm information concerning the provenance of the British Museum animal head before 1868, but it was said by the dealer who sold it to have come from northern Italy. The Vienna head has been identified in the records of the collections of Ambras Castle near Innsbruck (1529-95).

Glossary of scientific techniques

GAS CHROMATOGRAPHY-MASS SPECTROMETRY (GC/MS)

GC/MS is used to identify organic materials such as resins, fats and waxes from their chemical composition. The technique requires a sample to be taken but this can be very small, often no larger than a pin-head. Gas chromatography (GC) separates the different chemical components. The mass spectrometer (MS) then supplies a unique 'mass spectrum' for each compound, enabling it to be identified. From the suite of chemical components present the material can be traced to its botanical or zoological source, though it is not usually possible to identify exact species. Mixtures of materials can be identified, and chemical changes brought about by heating or degradation can also be observed.

OPTICAL MICROSCOPY

The optical microscrope contains one or more lenses that produce an enlarged image of the object placed in the focal plane of the lenses. The range of magnifications enables materials and surfaces to be identified or characterized.

RADIOGRAPHY

Radiography is particularly useful in museums because it is non-destructive. When an object is radiographed, radiation (typically X-rays, but also gamma-rays, neutrons or electrons) is passed into it. Some of the radiation is absorbed, some scattered and some may pass through to produce an image on photographic film or xeroradiograph plate placed behind the object. The amount of radiation that passes through will depend on several factors, including the energy of the radiation and the composition and thickness of the object. Thus it is possible to see the internal structure and identify breaks, joins, inlays of different materials and enclosed objects: internal details of an object that would otherwise be invisible.

RAMAN SPECTROSCOPY

Raman spectroscopy works by directing a laser beam onto the surface of the object. Most of this light is reflected from the sample unchanged, but a very small proportion interacts with the molecules in the material and its wavelength is changed. This is known as the Raman effect and the light scattered in this way is collected to produce a spectrum. Each material has a unique spectrum that can be used to identify the sample.

SCANNING ELECTRON MICROSCOPY (SEM)

The scanning electron microscope shows very detailed three-dimensional images at much higher magnifications than is possible with an optical microscope. It can focus on both the 'hills' and the 'valleys' of an object at the same time, so that sharp images of very fine details are produced. However, because the object is viewed in a beam of electrons, rather than light, it appears in shades of grey. As the beam of electrons scans backwards and forwards across the surface of a sample, different signals are produced. Electrons provide the magnified image of the surface. X-rays are also produced, and the X-ray spectrum, which is rather similar to that produced in X-ray fluorescence analysis (XRF), gives the composition of the area being examined.

X-RAY DIFFRACTION ANALYSIS (XRD)

X-ray diffraction is a powerful (almost) non-destructive technique for characterizing crystalline materials. When X-rays are fired at a crystalline sample some are diffracted by the regular crystal structure. In an X-ray camera, these diffracted X-rays produce a pattern of lighter and darker lines on the film. Every crystalline substance has a unique pattern and, by reference to standard data, a wide variety of materials can be identified. Unlike techniques such as XRF and other methods of chemical analysis that provide information on elemental composition, XRD allows a particular mineral to be identified.

X-RAY FLUORESCENCE ANALYSIS (XRF)

X-ray fluorescence is a technique of chemical analysis. It is non-destructive and often the complete object is placed in the sample chamber for analysis, avoiding the need to remove samples. The technique involves aiming an X-ray beam at the surface of an object; this beam is about 2 mm or less in diameter. The interaction of X-rays with an object causes secondary (fluorescent) X-rays to be generated. Each element present in the object produces X-rays with different energies. These X-rays can be detected and displayed as a spectrum of intensity against energy: the positions of the peaks identify which elements are present and the peak heights identify how much of each element is present. XRF is accurate and fast (a result can be obtained in a few minutes). It will quickly determine the alloy composition of a metal artefact and it can also be useful in the analysis of pigments.

Bibliography

ANAWALT, Patricia Rieff, 'They came to trade exquisite things: Ancient West Mexican–Ecuadorian contacts', in Richard F. Townsend (ed.), *Ancient West Mexico: Art and Archaeology of the Unknown Past* (London, 1998), pp. 233–49

ANONYMOUS CONQUEROR, *Narrative of Some Things of New Spain and of the Great City of Temestitan, Mexico*, translated by Marshall H. Saville (New York, 1917)

ARNOLD, Dean E., and Bruce F. BOHOR, 'Attapulgite and Maya Blue', *Archaeology*, XXVIII (1975), pp. 23–9

BARRERA VÁSQUEZ, Alfredo, ed., *Diccionario Maya Cordemex* (Mérida, 1980)

BERDAN, Frances F., *The Aztecs of Central Mexico* (New York, 1982)

BERDAN, Frances, 'Aztec Society: economy, tribute and warfare', in Matos Moctezuma and Solis Olguín (2002), pp. 38–47

BERDAN, Frances F., and Patricia Rieff ANAWALT, *The Codex Mendoza*, 4 vols (Berkeley, 1992)

BERJONNEAU, Gerald, E. Delataille and J.-L. Sonnery, *Rediscovered Masterpieces of Mesoamerica: Mexico, Guatemala, Honduras* (Boulogne, 1985)

BLAKE, W. P., 'The chalchihuitl of the Ancient Mexicans: its locality and association, and its identity with turquois', *American Journal of Science*, XXV (1858), pp. 227–32

BOONE, Elizabeth, *Stories in Red and Black* (Austin, 2000)

BYLAND, Bruce, 'Introduction and commentary', in G. Diaz and A. Rodgers, *The Codex Borgia* (New York, 1993), pp. xiii–xxxii

CARMICHAEL, Elizabeth, *Turquoise Mosaics from Mexico* (London, 1970)

CARRASCO, David, *Quetzalcoatl and the Irony of Empire* (Chicago, 1982)

CARTWRIGHT, C.R., 'Shell and Stone Tools', in P.L. Drewett, *Archaeological Survey of Barbados: Second Interim Report, Journal of the Barbados Museum and Historical Society*, xxxviii (1988), pp. 196–204

CASO, Alfonso, 'Lapidary work, goldwork and copperwork from Oaxaca' in R. Wauchope (ed.) *Handbook of Middle American Indians*, vol. III, part II (Austin, 1965), pp. 896–930

CASO, Alfonso, 'El tesoro de Monte Albán', *Memorias del Instituto Nacional de Antropología*, 13 (1969)

COBEAN, Robert H. and Alba Guadalupe MASTACHE, 'Turquoise and shell offerings in the Palacio Quemada of Tula, Hidalgo, Mexico', in D. K. Jansen and E. K. de Bock (eds), *Colecciones Latinoamericanas / Latin American Collections: Essays in Honour of Ted J. J. Leyenaar* (Leiden, 2003), pp. 51–65; see p. 57

COBEAN, Robert H. and Alba Guadalupe MASTACHE, *Las ofrendas del Palacio Quemado: turques y concha en un palacio Tolteca* (Albuquerque, n.d.)

CODEX FEJÉRVÁRY-MAYER: *12014 M City of Liverpool Museums* (Graz, 1971)

CODEX MAGLIABECHIANO: *The Book of the Life of the Ancient Mexicans … An Anonymous Hispano-Mexican Manuscript*, facsimile, with introduction, translation and commentary by Zelia Nuttall (Berkeley, 1903)

CODEX TELLERIANO-REMENSIS, facsimile in *Antigüadades de Mexico*, 4 vols (Mexico, 1964–7), vol. 1, pp. 151–338

CODEX VATICANUS A (3738-Codex-Ríos), in Viscount Kingsborough (ed.), *Antiquities of Mexico, Comprising Facsimiles of Ancient Mexican Paintings and Hieroglyphs*, 9 vols (London, 1831–48), vol. 1

CODEX ZOUCHE–NUTTALL: *The Codex Nuttall, a Picture Manuscript from Ancient Mexico: The Peabody Museum Facsimile*, ed. Zelia Nuttall with new introductory text by A.G. Miller (New York, 1975)

COE, M.D., *Mexico* (London, 1994)

COE, M.D. and R. A. DIEHL, *In the Land of the Olmec* (Austin, 1980)

COGGINS, Clemency Chase, and Orrin C. SHANE III, *Cenote de Sacrifice: Maya Treasures from the Sacred Well at Chichén Itzá* (Austin, 1984)

CORTÉS, Hernán, *Letters of Cortes: The Five Letters of Relation from Fernando Cortes to the Emperor Charles V*, translated by F. A. MacNutt (New York and London, 1908)

DALLAS MUSEUM OF ART: *A Guide to the Collection* (Dallas, 1997)

DRESSLER, R.L., 'Pre-Columbian Plants', *Botanical Museum Leaflets 16*, no. 6 (1953)

DRUCKER, Philip, Robert F. Heizer and Robert Squire, *Excavations at La Venta, Tabasco, 1955*, Bureau of American Ethnology, Bulletin 170 (Washington DC, 1959)

DURÁN, Diego, *The History of the Indies of New Spain (1581)*, translated, annotated, and with an introduction by Doris Heyden (Norman, 1994)

DÜRER, Albrecht, *Dürer's Record of Journeys to Venice and the Low Countries*, translated by Roger Fry (London, 1995)

EVANS, Susan Toby, *Ancient Mexico and Central America: Archaeology and Culture History* (London, 2004)

FEEST, Christian, *Vienna's Mexican Treasures: Aztec, Mixtec and Tarascan Works from the 16th Century Austrian Collections* (Vienna, 1990)

FIELDS, Virginia, and Dorie REENTS-BUDET, *The Origins of Sacred Maya Kingship* (Los Angeles, 2005)

FIELDS, Virginia, and Victor ZAMUDIO-TAYLOR (eds), *The Road to Aztlan: Art from a Mythic Homeland* (Los Angeles, 2001)

FLORESCANO, Enrique, *The Myth of Quetzalcoatl*, translated by Lysa Hochroth (London, 1999)

FREIDEL, A., L. Schele and J. Parker, *Maya Cosmos: Three Thousand Years on the Shaman's Path* (New York, 1993)

GRAULICH, Michel, *Myths of Ancient Mexico*, translated by Ortiz de Montellano and Thelma Ortiz de Montellano (Norman, 1997)

HARBOTTLE, Garman, and Phil WEIGAND, 'Turquoise in Pre-Columbian America', *Scientific American*, 266 (1992), pp. 78–85

HERNANDEZ, Francisco, *Historia de las Plantas de Nueva Espana* (Mexico City, 1943)

HOWES, F.N., *Vegetable Gums and Resins* (Waltham MA, 1949)

IXTLILXOCHITL, Fernando de Alva, *Obras históricas de don Fernando de Alva Ixtlilxochitl*, ed. Alfredo Chavero, 2 vols (Mexico, 1891–2)

JOSÉ-YACAMAN, M., Luis Rendón, J. Arenas and Mari Carmen Serra Puche, 'Maya Paint: and ancient nanostructured material ', *Science*, 273 (1996), pp. 223–5

KAVANAGH, G., 'Ancient Mexican Turquoise', unpublished MSc thesis, Institute of Archaeology, University of London (1987)

KING, J.C.H., 'Franks and Ethnography ', in Marjorie Caygill and John Cherry (eds), *A.W. Franks: Nineteenth-Century Collecting and the British Museum* (London, 1997), pp. 136–59

LA NIECE, S., and N. MEEKS, 'Diversity of Goldsmithing Traditions in the Americas and the Old World', in C. McEwan (ed.) *Precolumbian Gold: Technology, Style and Iconography* (London, 2000), pp. 220–39

LEHMANN, Walter, 'Altmexikanische Mosaiken und die Geschenke König Montecuzomas an Cortés', *Globus*, 90 (1906), pp. 318–22

LOCKE, Adrian, 'Gods of Death', in Matos Moctezuma and Solis Olguín (2002), pp. 205–6

LÓPEZ DE GÓMARA, Francisco, *Cortés: The Life of the Conqueror by his Secretary*, translated and edited by Lesley Byrd Simpson from the Spanish *Historia de la conquista de Mexico*, printed in Zaragoza, 1552 (Berkeley and Cambridge, 1964)

LÓPEZ LUJÁN, Leonardo, *The Offerings of the Templo Mayor of Tenochititlan*, translated by B.R. Oritz de Montellano and T. Ortiz de Montellano (Niwot CO, 1994)

LÓPEZ LUJÁN, Leonardo, 'The Aztec's Search for the Past', in Matos Moctezuma and Solis Olguín (2002), pp. 22–9

MCEWAN, Colin, *Ancient Mexico in the British Museum* (London, 1994)

MAGAR MEURS, Valerie, Luisa Maria Mainou and Patricia Meehan Hermanson, 'Estudio y Conservación del Disco de Mosaico de Turquesa de la Ofrenda 1', in Robert H. Cobean and Alba Guadalupe Mastache (eds), *Ofrendas en un Palacio Tolteca: Turquesa y Concha en el Palacio Quemado de Tula, Hidalgo* (Mexico City, n.d.)

MARCOS, Jorge G., 'Cruising to Acapulco and Back with the Thorny Oyster Set', *Journal of the Steward Anthropological Society*, IX/1–2 (1977–8), pp. 99–132

MARTIN, Simon, and Nikolai GRUBE, *Chronicle of the Maya Kings and Queens* (London, 2000)

MARTINEZ-CORTES, Fernando, *Pegamentos, gomas y resinas en el México prehispánico* (Mexico City, 1970)

MARTINEZ DONJUÁN, G., 'Los Olmecas en el estado de Guerrero', in John E. Clark (ed.), *Los Olmecas en Mesoamérica* (Mexico City, 1994), pp. 143–63

MARTYR D'Anghera, P., *De Orbe Novo: The Eight Decades of Peter Martyr D'Anghera*, translated by F.A. McNutt (New York and London, 1912)

MASON, J.A., 'Turquoise mosaics from northern Mexico', *Museum Journal* (1929)

MASTACHE, Alba Guadalupe, and Robert H. COBEAN, 'Ancient Tollan: the sacred precinct ', *RES*, 38 (autumn 2000), pp. 100–33

MATHIEN, F.J., 'Neutron Activation of Turquoise Artifacts from Chaco Canyon, New Mexico', *Current Anthropology*, XXII (1981), pp. 293–4

—, 'The Organization of Turquoise Production by the Prehistoric Chacoans', *American Antiquity*, LXVI (2001), pp. 103–18

MATOS MOCTEZUMA, Eduardo, *The Great Temple of the Aztecs* (London, 1988)

MATOS MOCTEZUMA, Eduardo, and Felipe SOLIS OLGUÍN, *Aztecs*, exh. cat., Royal Academy of Arts (London, 2002)

MAUDSLAY, Alfred P., *Biologia Centrali-Americana: or Contributions to the Knowledge of the Fauna and Flora of Mexico and Central America*, ed. F. Ducane Godman and Salvin Osbert, 5 vols (London, 1889–1902), vol. III Plates

MEYLAN, B.A., and B.G. Butterfield, *The Three-Dimensional Structure of Wood* (London, 1972)

MILLER, M., *The Art of Mesoamerica* (London, 2001)

MILLER, Mary and Simon MARTIN, *Courtly Art of the Ancient Maya* (London, 2004)

MILLER, M., and K. TAUBE, *The Gods and Symbols of Ancient Mexico and the Maya: An Illustrated Dictionary of Mesoamerican Religion* (London, 1993)

MILLS, John S., and Raymond WHITE, *The Organic Chemistry of Museum Objects* (Oxford, 1994)

MONTERO, S.A., 'Restoration of Turquoise Masks from Coixtlahuaca and Zaachila, Oaxaca', *Studies in Conservation*, 14 (1968), pp. 102–4

MORÁN-ZENTENO, D., *The Geology of the Mexican Republic*, translated by J.L. Wilson and Luis Sanchez-Barreda (Tulsa, 1994)

MOTTE-FRORAC, Elizabeth, 'Medicinal Use of Special Pine Resin among the P'urhépecha (Mexico)', in S.K. Jain (ed.), *Ethnobiology in Human Welfare* (New Delhi, 1996), pp. 223–32.

OVIEDO y Valdés, Gonzalo Fernández de, *Historia general y natural de las Indias, islas y tierra-firme del mar océano* (Madrid, 1851–5)

PANCZNER, W.D., *Minerals of Mexico* (New York, 1987)

PASZTORY, Esther, *Aztec Art* (New York, 1983)

—, 'The problem of the aesthetics of abstraction for pre-Columbian art and its implications for other cultures', *RES*, 19/20 (1990/1991), pp. 104–36

PAULSEN, Allison C., 'The Thorny Oyster and the Voice of God:

Spondylus and *Strombus* in Andean prehistory', *American Antiquity*, xxxix/4 (1974), pp. 597–607

PILLSBURY, Joanne, 'The Thorny Oyster and Origins of Empire: Implications of Recently Uncovered *Spondylus* imagery from Chan Chan', *American Antiquity* (1994), pp. 313–40

POGUE, Joseph E., *The Turquois: A Study of its History, Mineralogy, Geology, Ethnology, Archaeology, Mythology, Folklore, and Technology* (Washington DC, 1915)

POHL, John M.D., *The Politics of Symbolism in the Mixtec Codices* (Nashville, 1994)

—, 'Chichimecatlalli: strategies for cultural and commercial exchange between Mexico and the American Southwest, 1100–1521', in Fields and Zamudio-Taylor (Los Angeles, 2001), pp. 86–101

POLETTE, Lori A., George Meitzner, Miguel Jose Yacaman and Russell R. Chianelli, 'Maya Blue: application of XAS and HRTEM to materials science in art and archaeology', *Microchemical Journal*, 71 (2002), pp. 167–74

POSTER, A and FANE, D., *Guennol Collection: Cabinet of Wonders* (Brooklyn, 2000)

READ, C.H., 'On an Ancient Mexican Headpiece Coated with Mosaic', *Archaeologia*, 14 (1895), pp. 383–98

SAHAGÚN, Bernardo de, *Florentine Codex: General History of the Things of New Spain*, translated and edited by Arthur J.O. Anderson and Charles E. Dibble, 12 books in 13 vols (Salt Lake City, 1950–82)

SAVILLE, Marshall H., *Turquoise Mosaic Art in Ancient Mexico*, Indian Notes and Monographs, no. 8, Museum of the American Indian, Heye Foundation (New York, 1922)

SCHMIDT, Peter S., 'Las máscaras de Oxkintok, Yucatán', *Archaeologia Mexicana 16* (2004) pp. 30–33

SELER, E., *Gesammelte Abhandlungen zur Amerikanischen Sprach- und Alterthumskunde*, 5 vols (Berlin, 1902–23), vol. 2 (1904)

SOLIS OLGUÍN, Felipe, 'Religion ', in Matos Moctezuma and Solis Olguín (2002), pp. 225–6

STACEY, R.J., C.R. Cartwright and C. McEwan, 'Chemical characterisation of ancient Mesoamerican "copal" resins: preliminary results', *Archaeometry*, 48 (2006), pp. 323–40

STANDLEY, Paul C., *Trees and Shrubs of Mexico*, Contributions from the United States National Herbarium 23, no. 3 (Washington DC, 1923)

STEELE, Janet F. and Ralph SNAVELY, 'Cueva Cheve Tablet', *Journal of Cave and Karst Studies 59*(1) (1997), pp. 26–32

TAUBE, Karl, 'The Iconography of Mirrors at Teotihuacán', in Janet Catherine Berlo (ed.), *Art, Ideology and the City of Teotihuacán* (Washington DC, 1992), pp. 169–204

TAUBE, Karl, 'The Mirrors of Offerings 1 and 2 of Sala 2 in the Palacio Quemada at Tula: An Iconographic Interpretation', in Robert H. Cobean and Alba Guadelupe Mastache (eds), *Ofrendas en un Palacio Tolteca: Turquesa y Concha en el Palacio Quemado de Tula, Hidalgo* (Mexico City, n.d.)

TOWNSEND, Richard F., *State and Cosmos in the Art of Tenochtitlán*, Dumbarton Oaks Studies in Pre-Columbian Art and Archaeology, no.20 (Washington DC, 1979)

TOWNSEND, Richard F., *The Aztecs* (London, 1992)

TYLOR, E.B., 'Description of three very rare specimens of an ancient Mexican mosaic work (in the collections of Henry Christy, Esq.)', Appendix 5 to *Anahuac: Or Mexico and the Mexicans, Ancient and Modern* (1861), pp. 337–9

VARGAS, E. (ed.), *Las mascaras de la Cueva de Santa Ana Teloxtoc*, Serie Antropología 105 UNAM (Mexico City, 1989)

WEIGAND, Phil, and Acelia García de WEIGAND, 'A Macroeconomic Study of the Relationships between the Ancient Cultures of the American Southwest and Mesoamerica', in Fields and Zamudio-Taylor (2001), pp. 184–95

WINTER, Marcus and Martha Carmona MACÍAS, *Tesoros de Oaxaca* (Oaxaca 2001)

YOUNG, S.M.M., D.A. Phillips and F.J. Mathien, 'Lead Isotope Analysis of Turquoise Sources in the Southwestern U.S.A. and Mesoamerica: a preliminary report', in S. Demirci, A.M. Özer and G.D. Summers (eds), *Archaeometry '94: Proceedings of the 29th International Symposium on Archaeometry* (Tübitak, 1994), pp. 147–50

Index

Picture Credits

All images prefixed by BM or provided by the Deparment of Scientific Research, British Museum, are © the Trustees of the British Museum.

Cover: (front) BM Am 1894-634; (back) BM Am ST 401

Chapter 1

p. 1: BM Am ST 401; p. 2: BM Am ST 400; p. 11: Firenze, Biblioteca Medicea Laurenziana, Sahagún, Bk 12, pl. 3, ill. 12. By permission of the Ministero per i Beni e le Attivita Culturali; p. 12: (from left to right) BM Am ST 400; BM Am 1894-634; BM Am ST 400a; BM Am ST 401; BM Am ST 397.a; BM Am + 6382; BM Am + 165; BM Am ST 399; BM Am Q87.3; p. 13: BM Am ST 401; p. 14: Dallas Museum of Art, The Roberta Coke Camp Fund; p. 15: Colin McEwan; p. 16: (left and right) Museo Nacional de Antropología Mexico City; p. 17: (left) Museo Nacional de Arqueología, Guatemala City, © Justin Kerr; (right) Museo de Antropología, Palacio Cantón, Mérida, Yucatán; p. 18: drawings (top) after Carmichael 1970; (bottom) after Miller 2001; p. 18: (right) Dumbarton Oaks, Pre-Columbian Collection, Washington DC; p. 19: (left) The Peabody Museum of Archaeology & Ethnology, Harvard University, Cambridge, Massachusetts, USA; (right) Colin McEwan; p. 20: BM Am 1825,12-10.11; p. 21: (left) BM Am Add. MS 39671; (right) Codex Magliabechiano, Firenze, Biblioteca Nazionale Centrale. By permission of the Ministero per i Bene e le Attivita Culturali; p. 23: Colin McEwan.

Chapter 2

pp. 24, 25: All images provided by the Department of Scientific Research, British Museum; p. 26: two images (top) provided by the Department of Scientific Research, British Museum; (bottom) BM Am ST 399; p. 27: Codex Mendoza folio 40r, illustrations the Bodleian Library, University of Oxford; centre and bottom image provided by the Department of Scientific Research, British Museum; p. 28: both images courtesy Phil Weigand; p. 29: (map) David Hoxley; p. 30: Firenze, Biblioteca Medicea Laurenziana, Sahagún, Bk 11, ill. 767. By permission of the Ministero per i Beni e le Attivita Culturali;

p. 32: (top) shell sample palettes provided by the Department of Scientific Research, British Museum; (centre left) Codex Mendoza folio 38r, the Bodleian Library, University of Oxford; (centre right) Marcus Coltro, Femorale.com; (bottom) Firenze, Biblioteca Medicea Laurenziana, Sahagún, Bk 11, ill. 198. By permission of the Ministero per i Beni e le Attiva Culturali; p. 33: BM 1894-634; p. 34: (top and bottom left) Firenze, Biblioteca Medicea Laurenziana, Sahagún, Bk 1, ill. 34 and Bk 11, ill. 377. By permission of the Ministero per i Beni e le Attiva Culturali; (right) provided by the Department of Scientific Research, British Museum; p. 35: provided by the Department of Scientific Research, British Museum; p. 36: (left) Wellcome Library, London; p. 38: (right) Codex Mendoza, British Museum; (bottom) Firenze, Biblioteca Medicea Laurenziana, Sahagún, Bk 9, ill. 68. By permission of the Ministero per i Beni e le Attiva Culturali; p. 39: (top) provided by the Department of Scientific Research, British Museum; (bottom) Firenze, Biblioteca Medicea Laurenziana, Sahagún, Bk 11, ill. 788. By permission of the Ministero per i Beni e le Attiva Culturali; p. 40: (left) Museo Nacional de Antropología, Mexico City / CONACULTA.-INAH.-MEX. Reproduction authorised by the 'Instituto Nacional de Antropología e Historia'; (right) provided by the Department of Scientific Research, British Museum; p. 41: (left) Codex Mendoza, folio 361, the Bodleian Library, University of Oxford; (right) BM Q87 Am.3.

Chapter 3

p. 42: BM Am Add. MS 39671; p. 43: Museo regional de Puebla, Mexico; p. 44: BM Am ST 400; p. 45: (details 60, 61, 63, 64) BM Am ST 400; Pinctada mother of pearl shell provided by the Department of Scientific Research, British Museum; p. 46: BM Am ST 400; p. 47: (left) BM Am 1849,6-29.1; (right) BM Am ST 400; pp. 48 and 49: BM Am Q78 Am.3; radiograph picture provided by the Department of Scientific Research, British Museum; p. 50: Michel Zabe/BMI CONACULTA.-INAH.-MEX; Reproduction authorised by the 'Instituto Nacional de Antropologia e Historia'; p. 51: (left) BM Ethno Q78 Am.3; (right) National Museum of Denmark, Copenhagen; p. 52: Am + 6382;

p. 53: (bottom) provided by the Department of Scientific Research, British Museum; p. 54: BM Am + 6382; p. 55: BM Am 1894-634; p. 56: BM Am 1894-634: p. 57: BM Am1894-634; p. 58: BM Am 1894-634; p. 59: (top) Firenze, Biblioteca Medicea Laurenziana, Sahagún, Florentine Codex, folio 74r. By permission of the Ministero per i Beni e le Attiva Culturali; (bottom) Firenze, Biblioteca Medicea Laurenziana, Sahagún, Bk 1, pl. 2, ill. 2. By permission of the Ministero per i Beni e le Attiva Culturali: p. 60: (top) BM Am ST 397.a; (bottom) © Museum for Völkerkunde/Wien; p. 61: Museo del Templo Mayor / CONACULTA.-INAH.-MEX; Reproduction authorised by the 'Istituto Nacional de Antropologia e Historia'. Photograph: German Zuniga and Froylan Ramos; p. 62: Musee royaux d'Art et d'Histoire (Brussels); p. 63: (left) illustration by Garth Denning; (right) Courtesy of The National Museum of the American Indian, Smithsonian Institution (10.8708), Washington DC; p. 64 (top) illustration after Read 1895; fig.4; illustration using BM Am ST 397.a; p. 65: BM Am ST 397.a; p. 66: (top and bottom) BM Am ST 397.a; p. 67: BM Am ST 40; p. 68: (left) National Museums of Liverpool; (right) BM Am Add. MS 39671; p. 69: Xeroradiographs all provided by the Department of Scientific Research, British Museum; pp. 70 and 71: BM Am ST 401; p. 72: Codex Magliabechiano, lam.66, Firenze, Biblioteca Nazionale Centrale. By permission of the Ministero per i Bene e le Attiva Culturali; p. 73: BM Am ST 399; p. 74: BM Am ST 399; p. 75: (top) BM Am Add. MS 39671; (bottom) Archivo fotografico del Museo Preistorico Etnografico L. Pigorini, Roma; p. 76: BM Am ST 399; p. 77: BM Ethno ST 399; pp. 78 and 79: BM Am + 165; p. 80: (left) BM Am + 165; (right) Museo Nacional de Antropología, Mexico City; p. 81: radiograph provided by the Department of Scientific Research, British Museum; p. 82: BM Am ST 400a; p. 83: radiograph provided by the Department of Scientific Research, British Museum; p. 84: BM Am ST 400a; p. 85: provided by the Department of Scientific Research, British Museum.